BOB DYLAN
GREATEST HITS
SONGTAB EDITION

D1302942

AMSCO PUBLICATIONS
NEW YORK/LONDON/SYDNEY

COMPILED BY LESLIE BARR
BACK COVER PHOTOGRAPHY BY KEN REGAN/CAMERA 5
SONGTAB ARRANGEMENTS BY MARCEL ROBINSON

THIS BOOK PUBLISHED 1992 BY AMSCO PUBLICATIONS,
A DIVISION OF MUSIC SALES CORPORATION, NEW YORK. NY.

ORDER NO. AM 87466
US INTERNATIONAL STANDARD BOOK NUMBER: 0.8256.1327.2
UK INTERNATIONAL STANDARD BOOK NUMBER: 0.7119.2862.2

EXCLUSIVE DISTRIBUTORS:
MUSIC SALES CORPORATION
257 PARK AVENUE SOUTH, NEW YORK, NY 10010
MUSIC SALES LIMITED
8/9 FRITH STREET, LONDON W1V 5TZ ENGLAND
MUSIC SALES PTY. LIMITED
120 ROTHSCHILD STREET, ROSEBERY, SYDNEY, NSW 2018, AUSTRALIA

PRINTED IN THE UNITED STATES OF AMERICA BY
VICKS LITHOGRAPH AND PRINTING CORPORATION

CONTENTS

EXPLANATION OF SYMBOLS AND TECHNIQUES

Right-Hand and Left-Hand Fingers

Left Hand   Right Hand

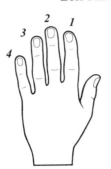
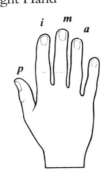

Tablature

Tablature is written on six lines. Each line represents a string of the guitar.

The 1st string (①) is the highest string; the 6th string (⑥) is the lowest.

Frets and open strings are indicated by numbers:

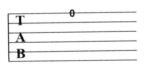      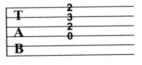

  open 1st string (①)   3rd fret, 2nd string   D chord

Hammeron:

   Indicates a hammeron with the left-hand finger hammering onto the second note. Only the first note is struck by the right hand.

Pulloff:

   Indicates a pulloff. The right hand strikes the first note and the left-hand finger pulls away to sound the second note. Only the first note is struck by the right hand.

Rhythm

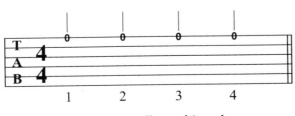

quarter notes, all equal in value

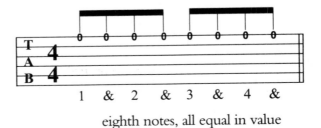

eighth notes, all equal in value

Ties:

A tie indicates that only the 1st note is played and is held for the value of the 2nd note.

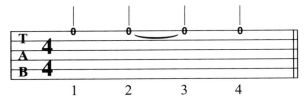
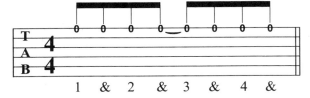

Beat 2 is played and held through the value of beat 3. Beat 3 is not played.

The note on beat 3 is not played.

Strumming Patterns

↑ Denotes a downstroke. A downstroke is executed by striking all of the strings indicated, from low notes to high, with the nail of the index finger.

↓ Denotes an upstroke. An upstroke is a lighter stroke executed by touching only 1, 2, or 3 strings of the chord, from high notes to low, with the nail of the index finger.

Basic Strumming Patterns

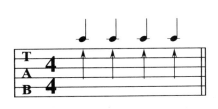
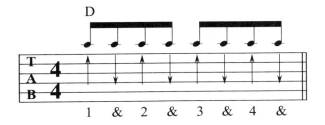

even downstrokes on a D chord

even upstrokes and downstrokes on a D chord

Syncopated Strumming Patterns

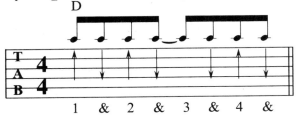
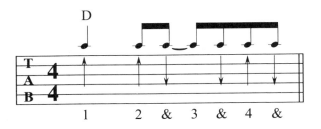

Leave out the downstroke on beat 3.

Leave out the upstroke after beat 1, and the downstroke on beat 3.

Leave out the upstroke after beat 1, the downstroke on beat 3, and the upstrokes after beat 4.

Strumming Patterns with Bass Note

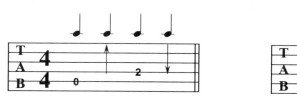

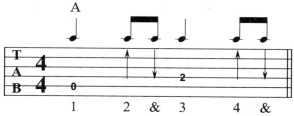

bass notes with chord strums,
using an A chord

with added upstrokes

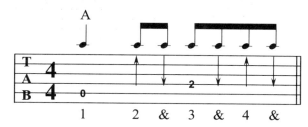

more added upstrokes

Fingerpicking Patterns

As a general rule the thumb *(p)* plays the bottom three (bass) strings with an occasional move to the 3rd string. The fingers *(i, m,* and *a)* play the top three (treble) strings.

simple arpeggio using open strings:

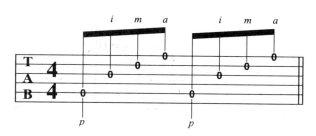

Try this with an A chord:

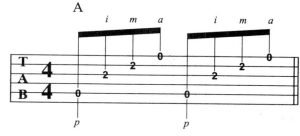

¾ time arpeggio using open strings:

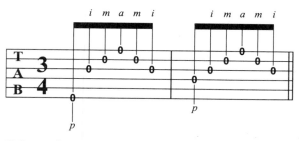

Try this using an Em chord:

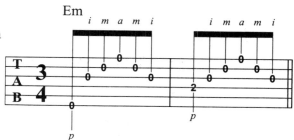

Rhumba or Syncopated Bass Pattern

using open strings:

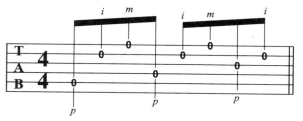

Try this using an Am chord:

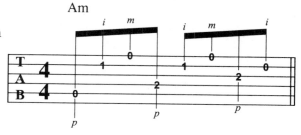

Travis Pick

In the next three examples the thumb and middle finger strike together. The remainder of the picking is exactly the same.

using open strings:

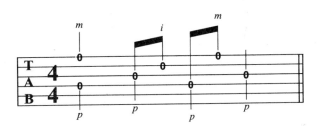

Try this with a D chord:

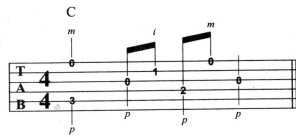

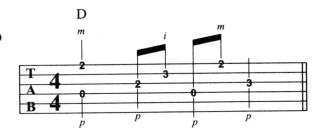

using open strings:

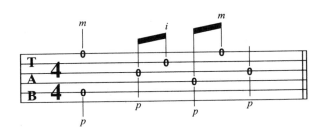

Now try it with a C chord:

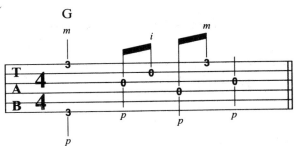

using open strings:

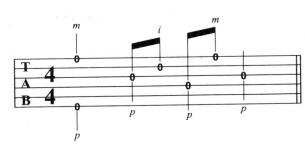

And with a G chord:

Travis Pick with All Three Versions

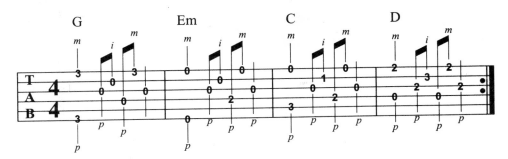

Blowin' In The Wind
(Version I)

Words and Music by Bob Dylan

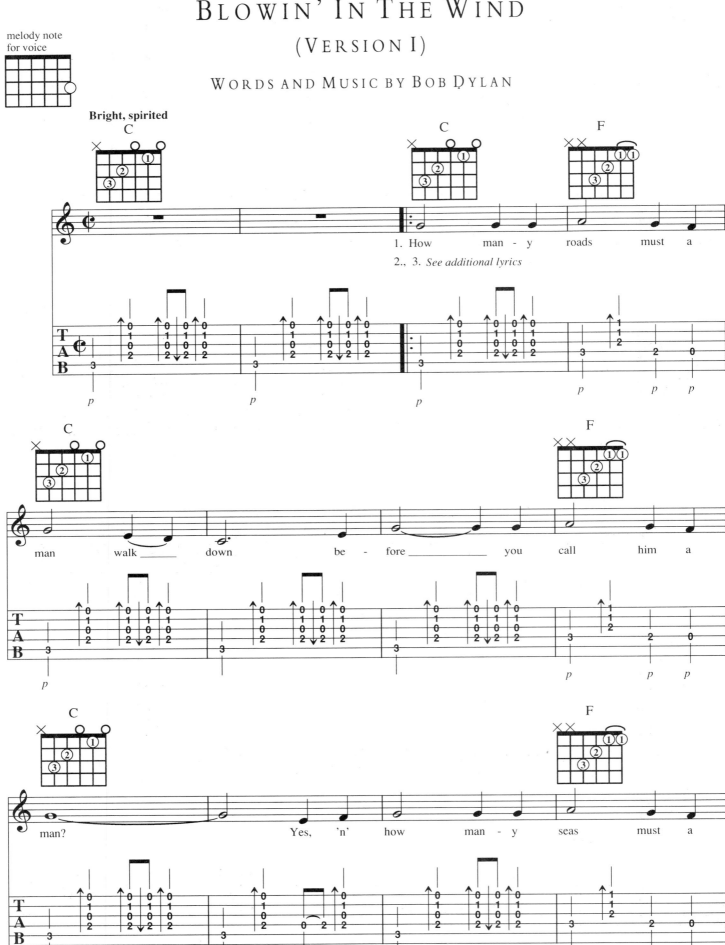

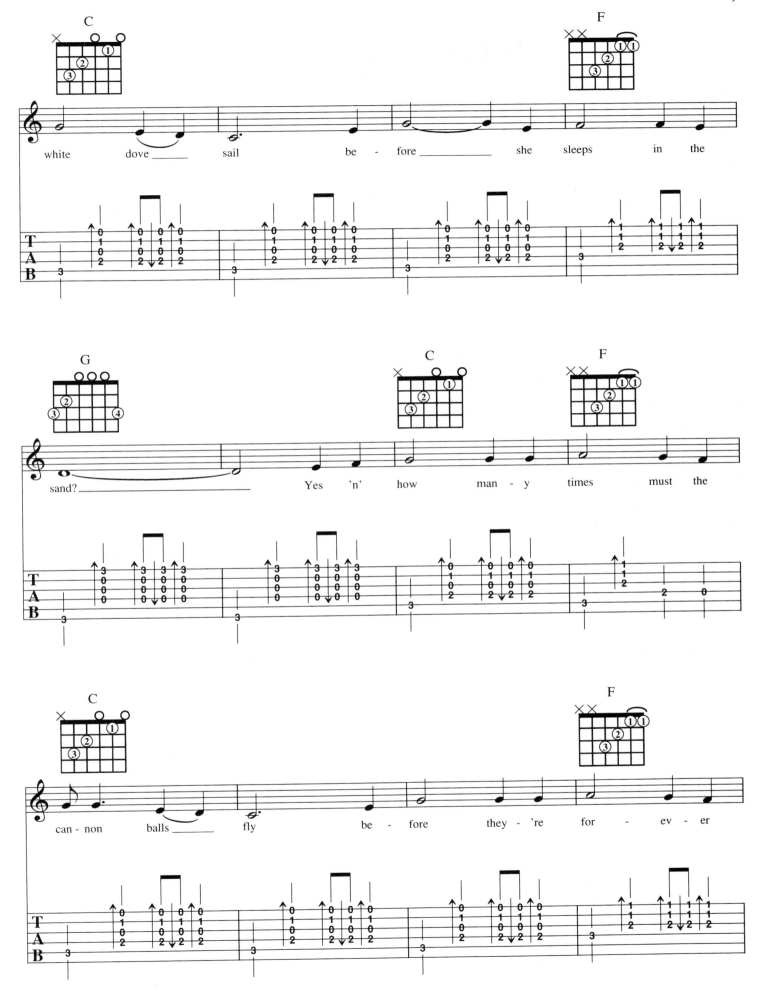

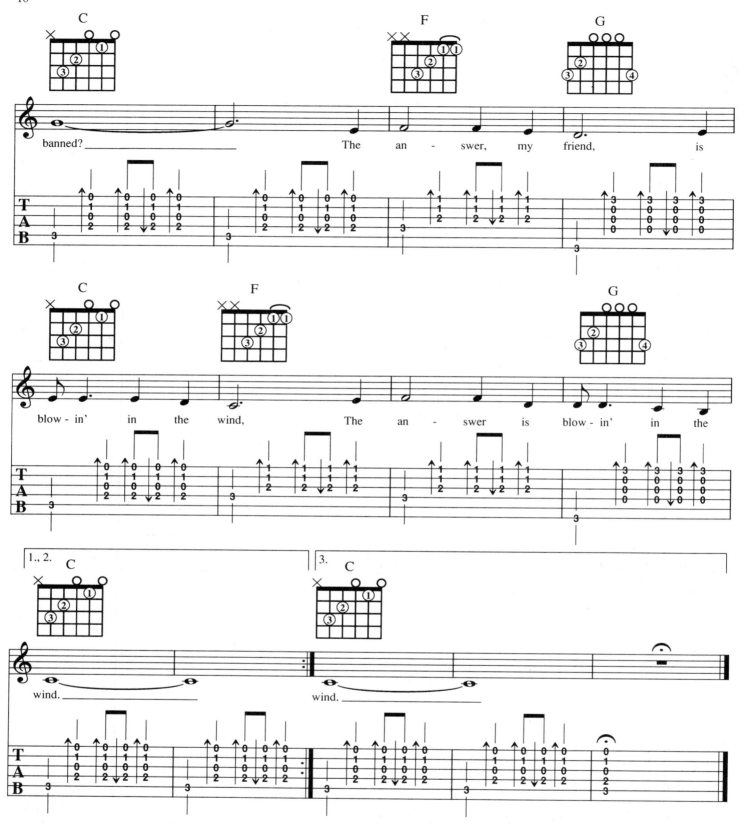

Additional lyrics

2. How many years can a mountain exist
   before it's washed to the sea?
   Yes, 'n' how many years can some people exist
   before they're allowed to be free?
   Yes, 'n' how many times can a man turn his head,
   pretending he just doesn't see?
   The answer, my friend, is blowin' in the wind,
   The answer is blowin' in the wind.

3. How many times must a man look up
   before he can see the sky?
   Yes, 'n' how many ears must one man have
   before he can hear people cry?
   Yes, 'n' how many deaths will it take till he knows
   that too many people have died?
   The answer, my friend, is blowin' in the wind,
   The answer is blowin' in the wind.

BLOWIN' IN THE WIND
(VERSION II)

WORDS AND MUSIC BY BOB DYLAN

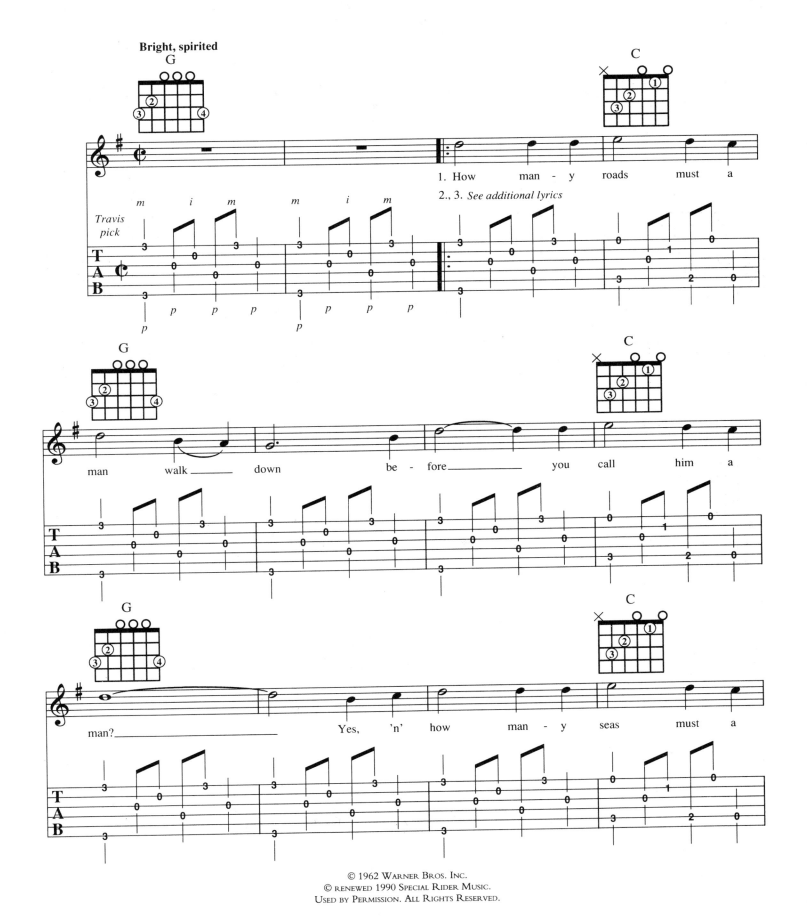

white   dove _____ sail   be - fore _____   she   sleeps   in   the

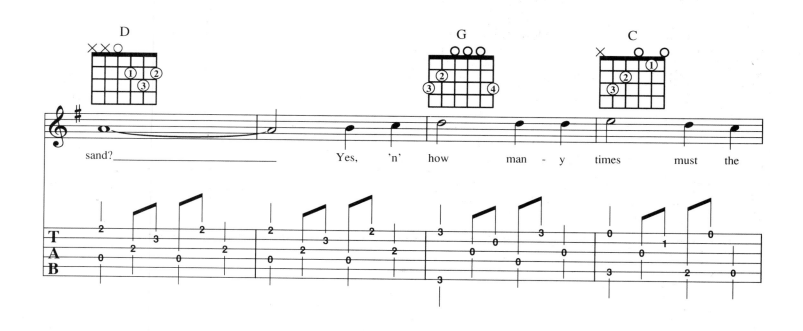

sand? _____   Yes, 'n' how   man - y   times   must   the

can - non - balls _____ fly   be - fore   they 're   for - ev - er

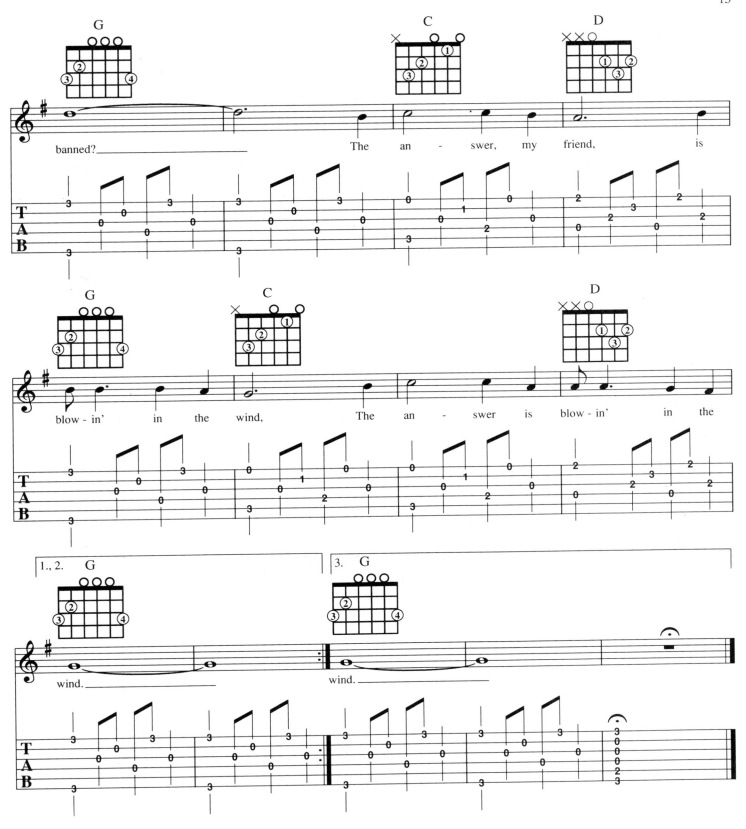

Additional lyrics

2. How many years can a mountain exist
   before it's washed to the sea?
   Yes, 'n' how many years can some people exist
   before they're allowed to be free?
   Yes, 'n' how many times can a man turn his head,
   pretending he just doesn't see?
   The answer, my friend, is blowin' in the wind,
   The answer is blowin' in the wind.

3. How many times must a man look up
   before he can see the sky?
   Yes, 'n' how many ears must one man have
   before he can hear people cry?
   Yes, 'n' how many deaths will it take till he knows
   that too many people have died?
   The answer, my friend, is blowin' in the wind,
   The answer is blowin' in the wind.

melody note
for voice

Boots Of Spanish Leather

Words and Music by Bob Dylan

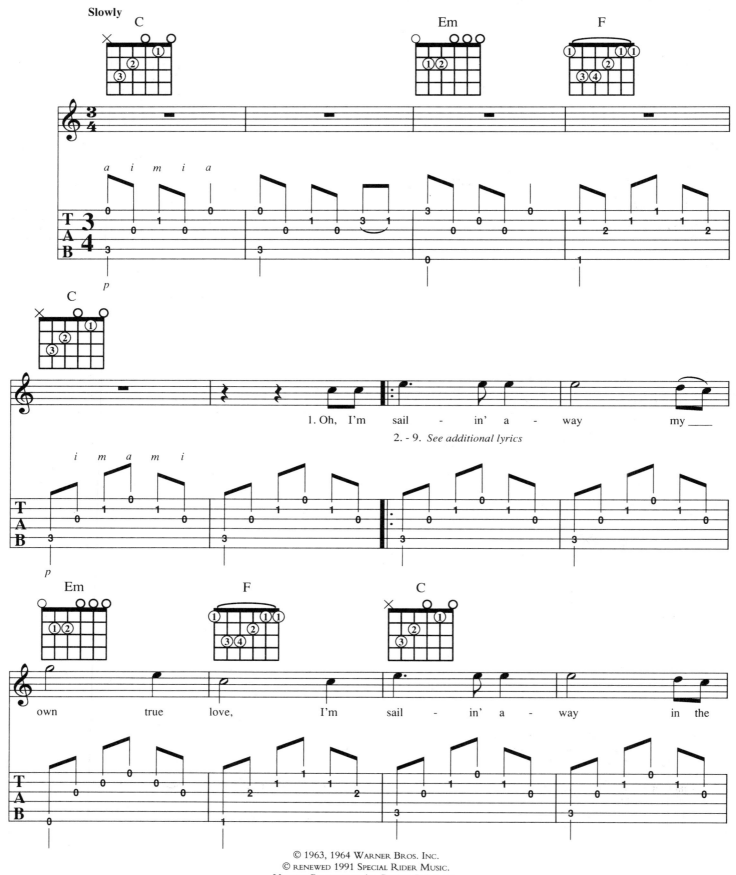

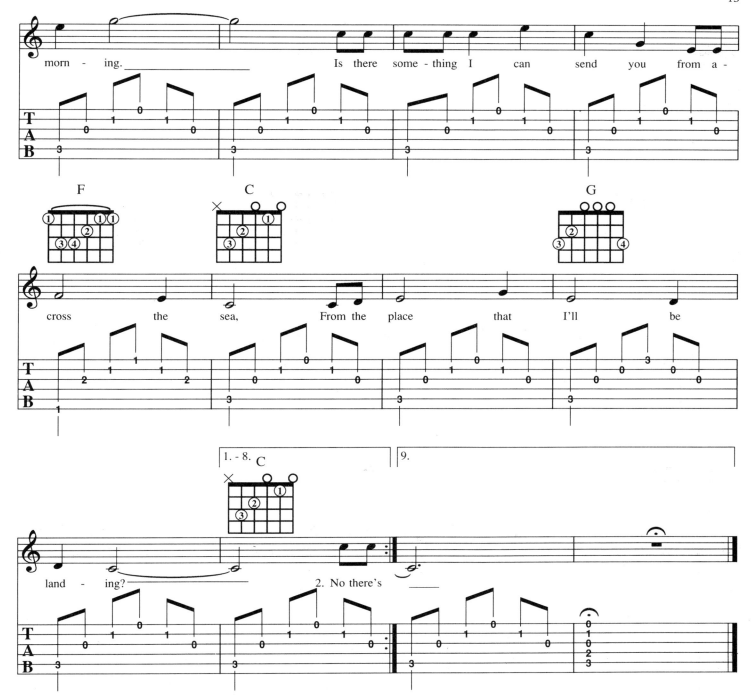

Additional lyrics

2. No there's nothin' you can send me, my own true love,
There's nothin' I wish to be ownin'.
Just carry yourself back to me unspoiled,
From across that lonesome ocean.

3. Oh, but I just thought you might want something fine
Made of silver or of golden,
Either from the mountains of Madrid
Or from the coast of Barcelona.

4. Oh but if I had the stars from the darkest night
And the diamonds from the deepest ocean,
I'd forsake them all for your sweet kiss,
For that's all I'm wishin' to be ownin'.

5. That I might be gone a long time
And it's only that I'm askin',
Is there somethin' I can send you to remember me by,
To make your time more easy passin'.

6. Oh, how can, how can you ask me again,
It only brings me sorrow.
The same thing I want from you today,
I would want again tomorrow.

7. I got a letter on a lonesome day,
It was from her ship a-sailin',
Saying I don't know when I'll be comin' back again,
It depends on how I'm a-feelin'.

8. Well, if you, my love, must think that-a-way,
I'm sure your mind is roamin'.
I'm sure your heart is not with me,
But with the country to where you're goin'.

9. So take heed, take heed of the western wind,
Take heed of the stormy weather,
And yes, there's something you can send back to me,
Spanish boots of Spanish leather.

Everything Is Broken

Words and Music by Bob Dylan

melody note
for voice

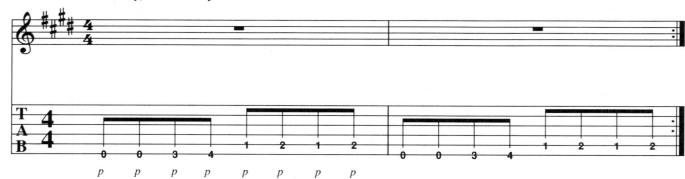

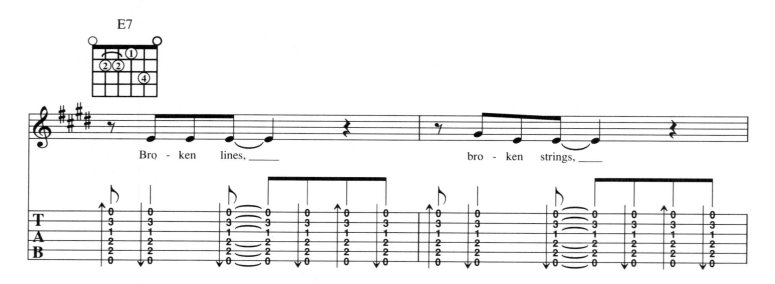

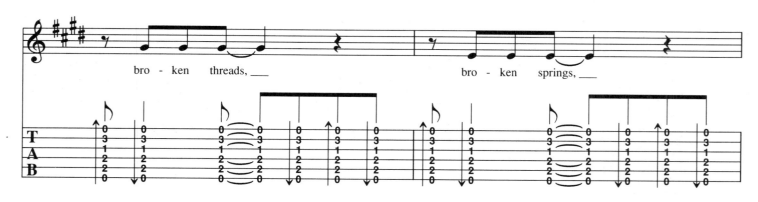

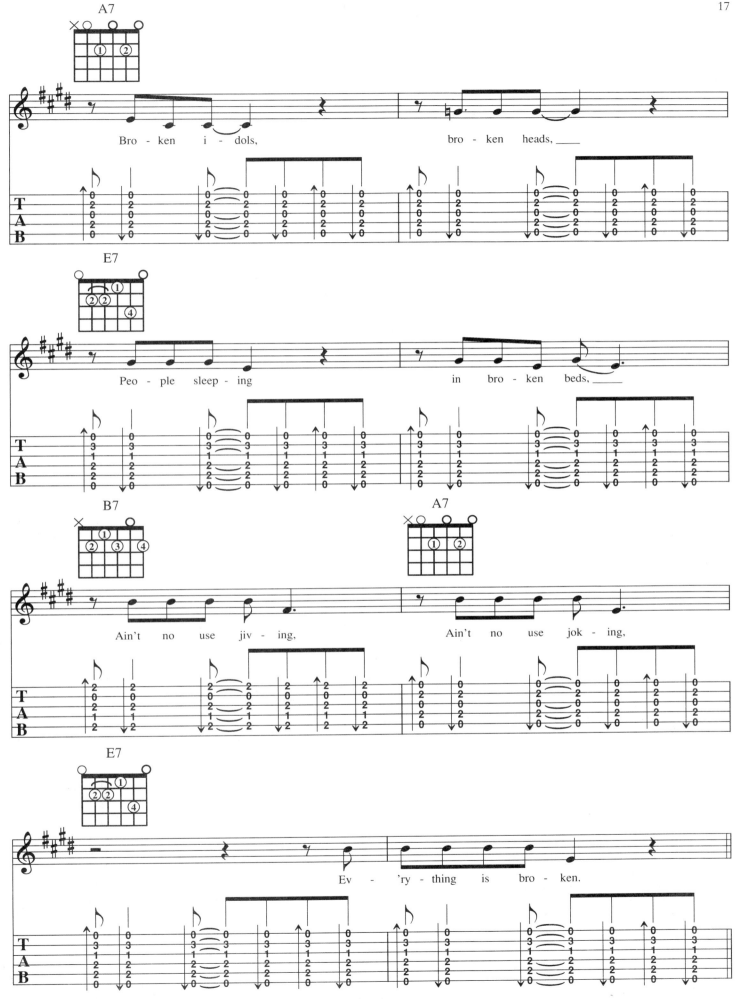

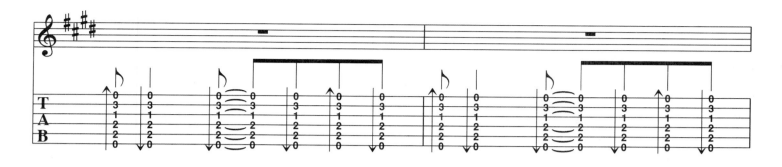

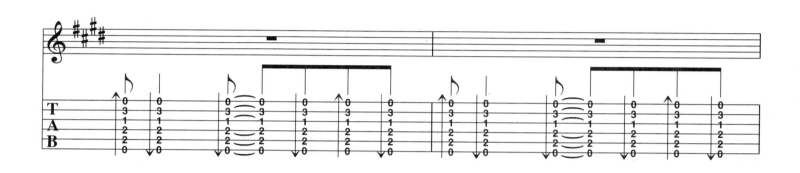

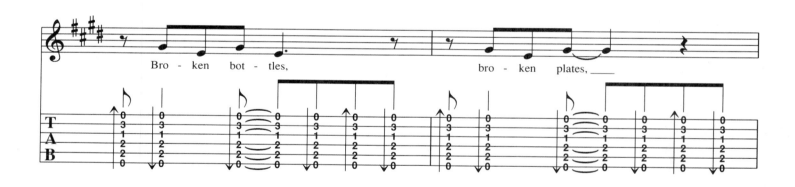

Bro - ken bot - tles,   bro - ken plates, _____

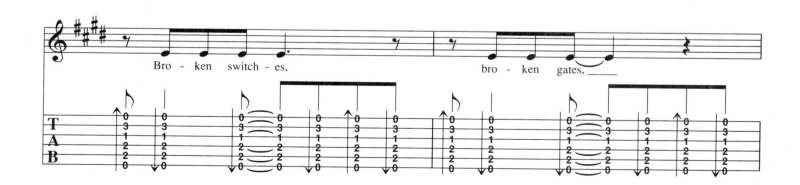

Bro - ken switch - es,   bro - ken gates, _____

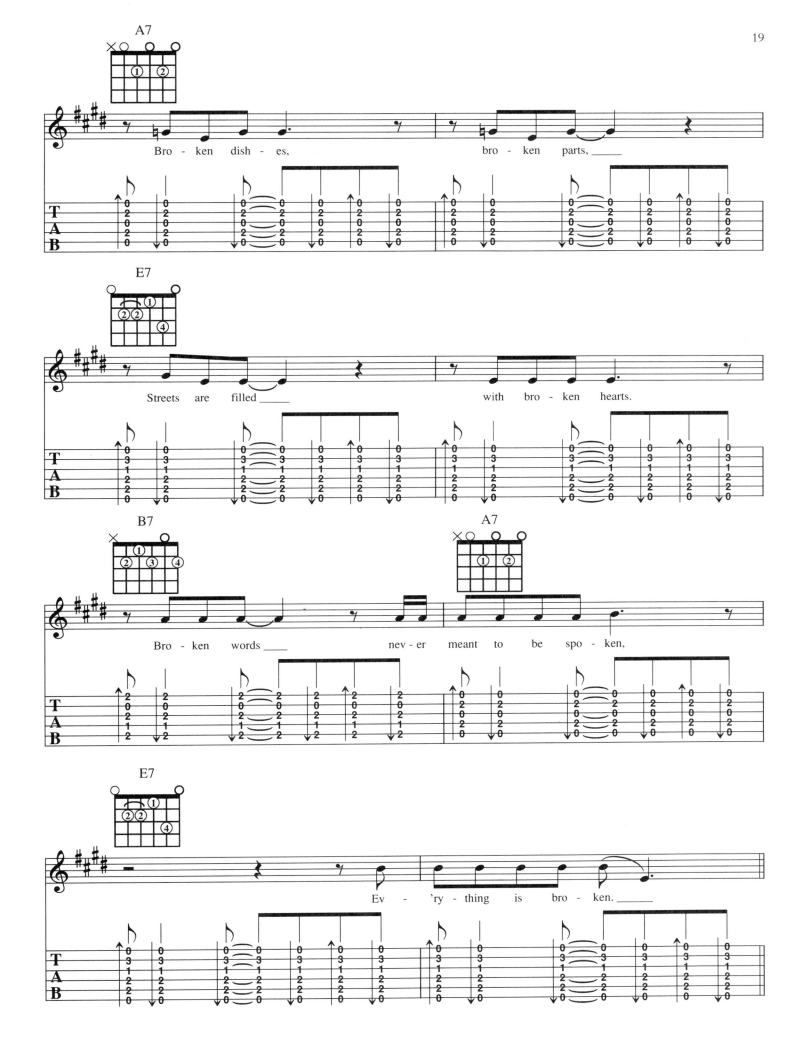

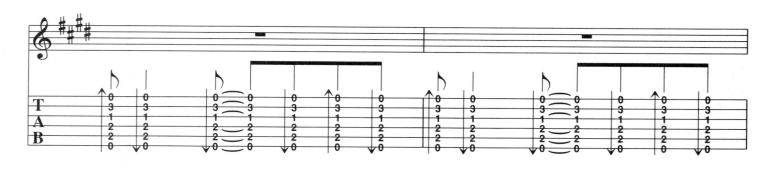

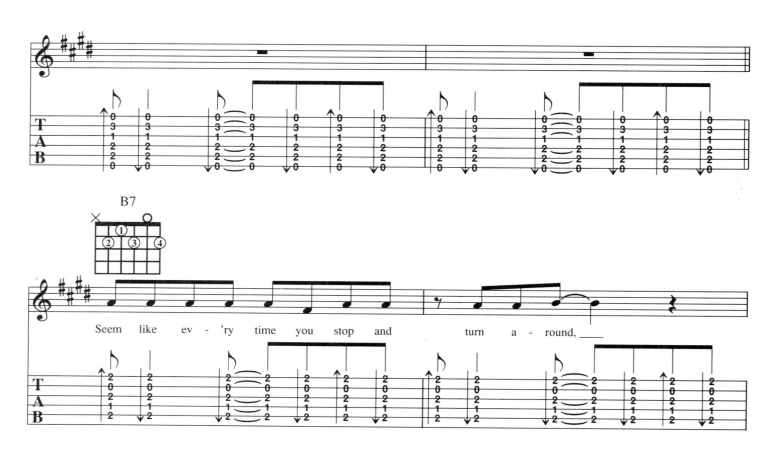

Seem like ev-'ry time you stop and turn a-round, ____

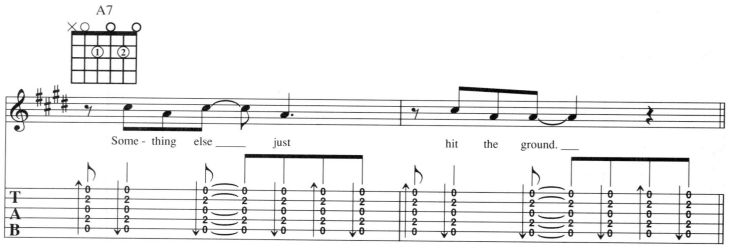

Some-thing else ____ just hit the ground. ___

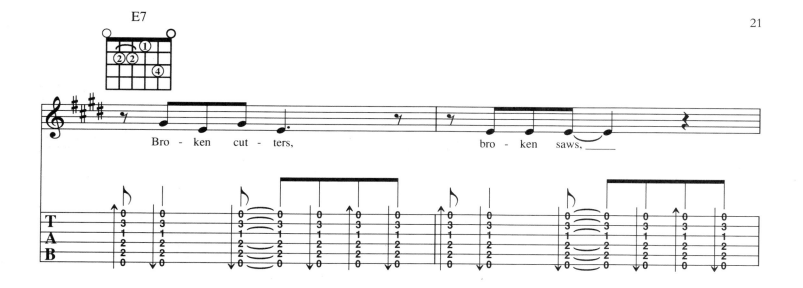

Bro - ken cut - ters, bro - ken saws, _____

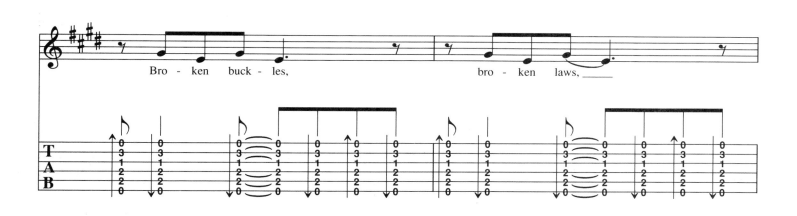

Bro - ken buck - les, bro - ken laws, _____

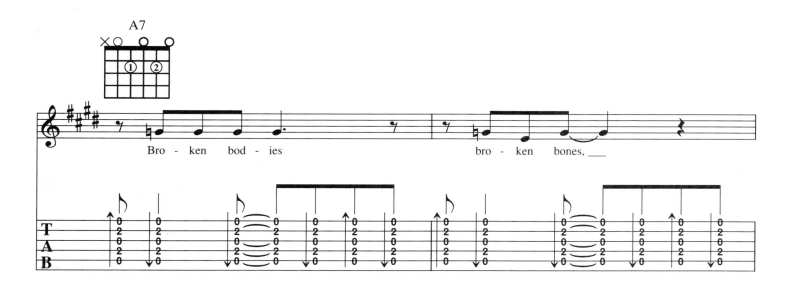

Bro - ken bod - ies bro - ken bones, ___

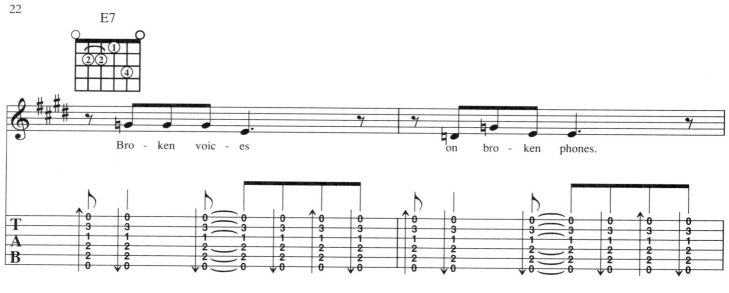

Bro - ken voic - es on bro - ken phones.

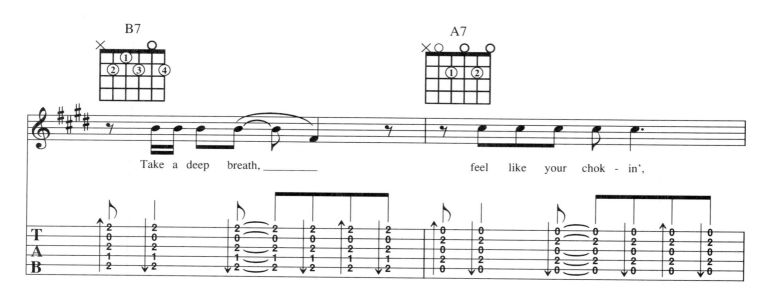

Take a deep breath, _____ feel like your chok - in',

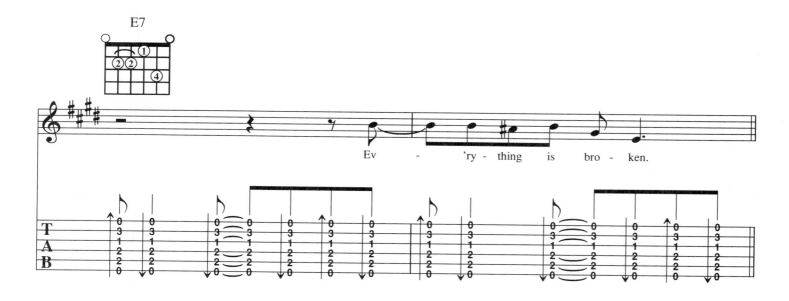

Ev - 'ry - thing is bro - ken.

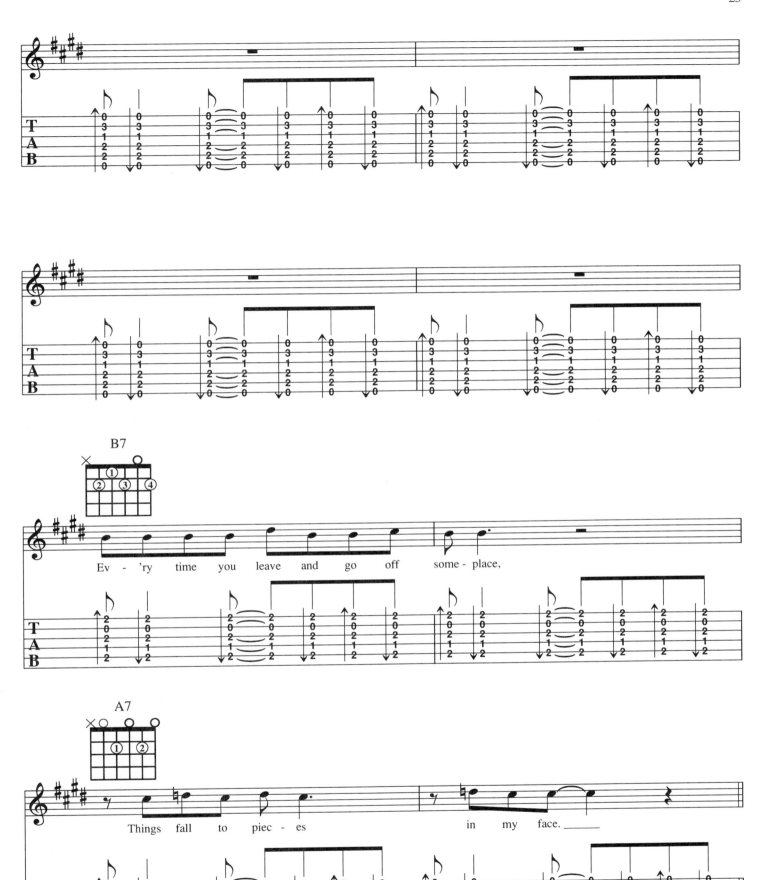

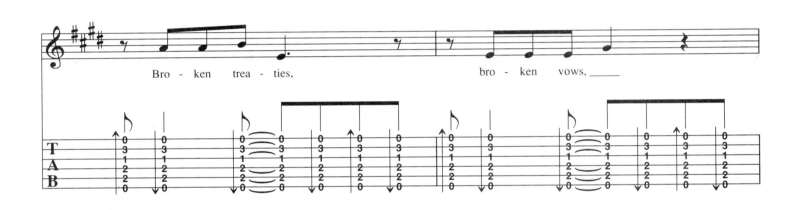

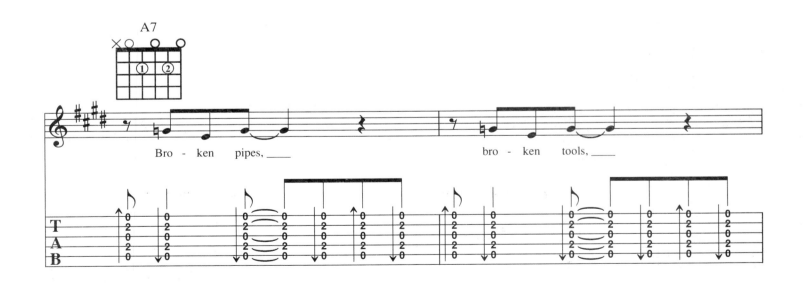

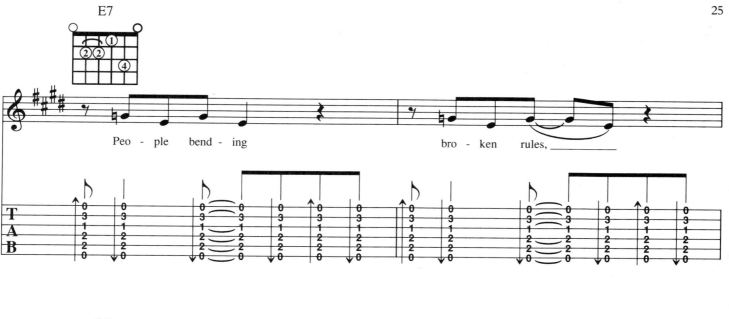

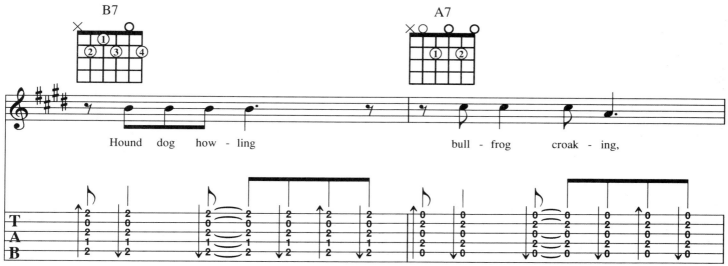

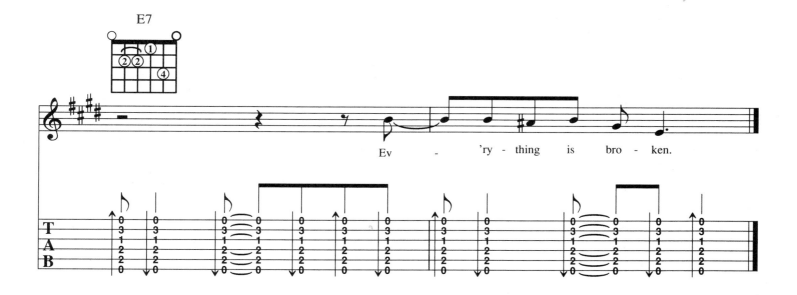

Don't Think Twice, It's All Right

Words and Music by Bob Dylan

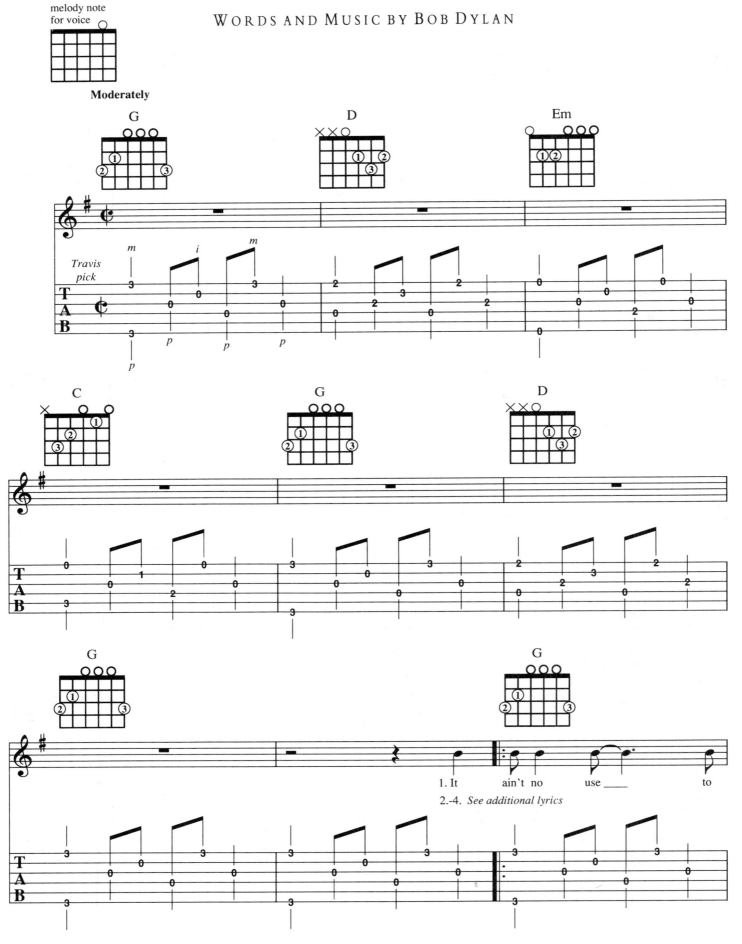

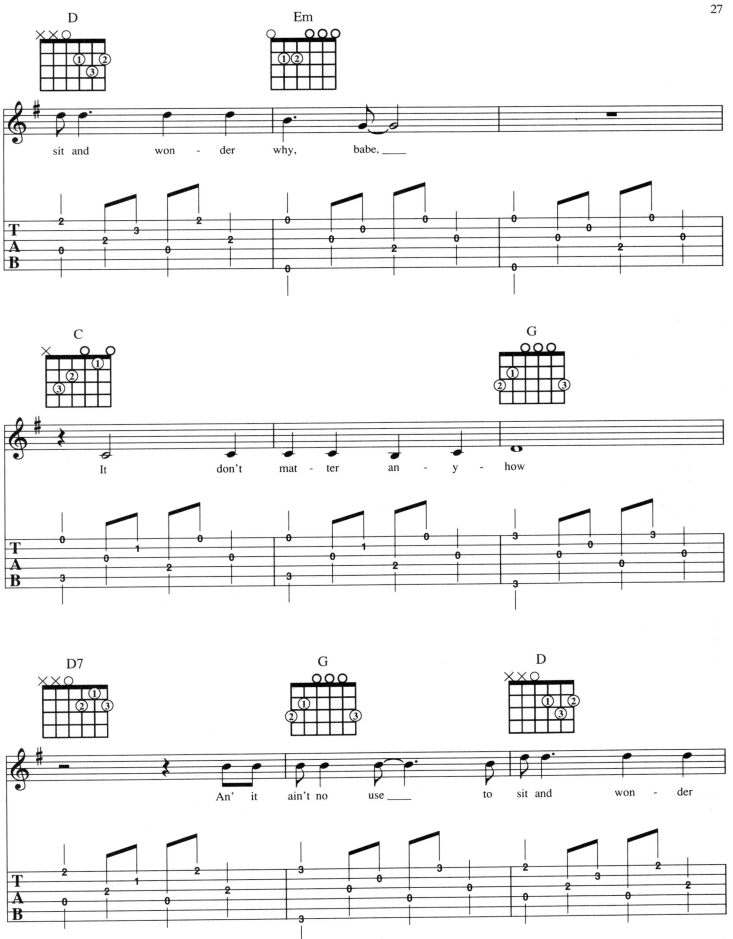

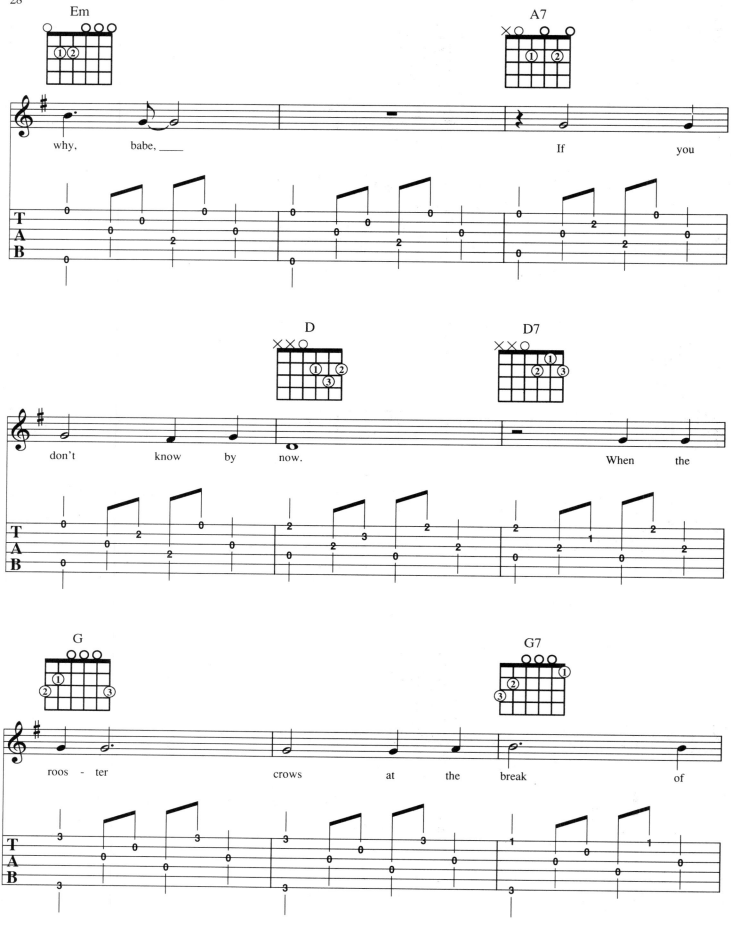

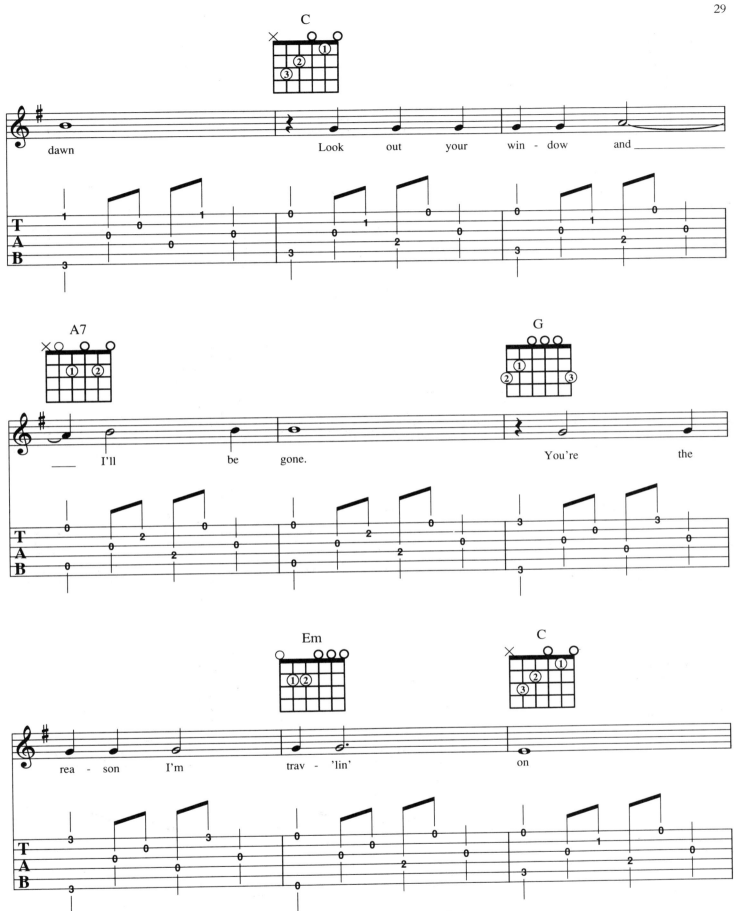

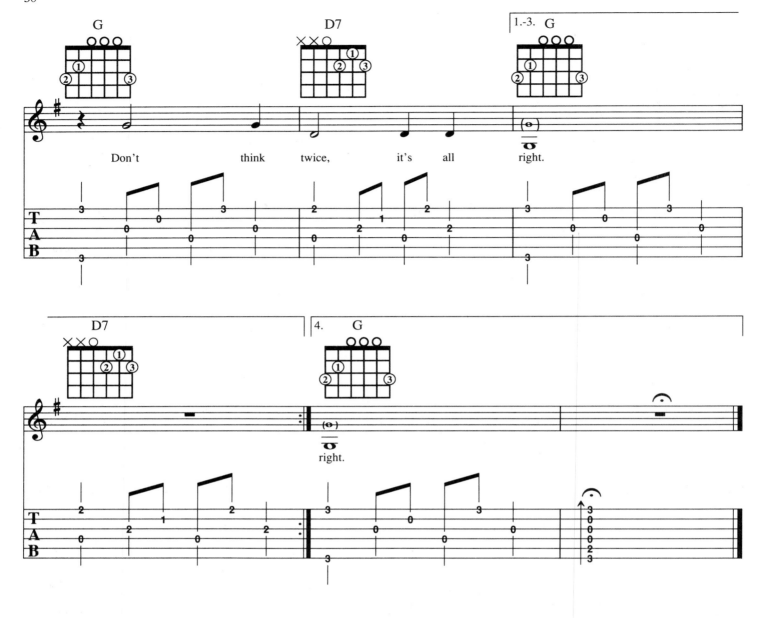

Don't think twice, it's all right.

right.

Additional lyrics

2. It ain't no use in turnin' on your light, babe,
   That light I never knowed.
   An' it ain't no use in turnin' on your light, babe,
   I'm on the dark side of the road.
   Still I wish there was somethin' you would do or say
   To try to make me change my mind and stay,
   We never did too much talkin' anyway,
   So don't think twice, it's all right.

3. It ain't no use in callin' out my name, gal,
   Like you never did before.
   It ain't no use in callin' out my name, gal.
   I can't hear you anymore.
   I'm a-thinkin' and a-wond'rin' all the way down the road,
   I once loved a woman, a child I'm told.
   I gave her my heart but she wanted my soul.
   But don't think twice it's all right.

4. I'm walkin' down that long lonesome road, babe,
   Where I'm bound I can't tell.
   But goodbye's too good a word, gal,
   So I'll just say fare thee well,
   I ain't sayin' you treated me unkind,
   You could have done better, but I don't mind.
   You just kinda wasted my precious time.
   But don't think twice it's all right.

A Hard Rain's A Gonna Fall

Words and Music by Bob Dylan

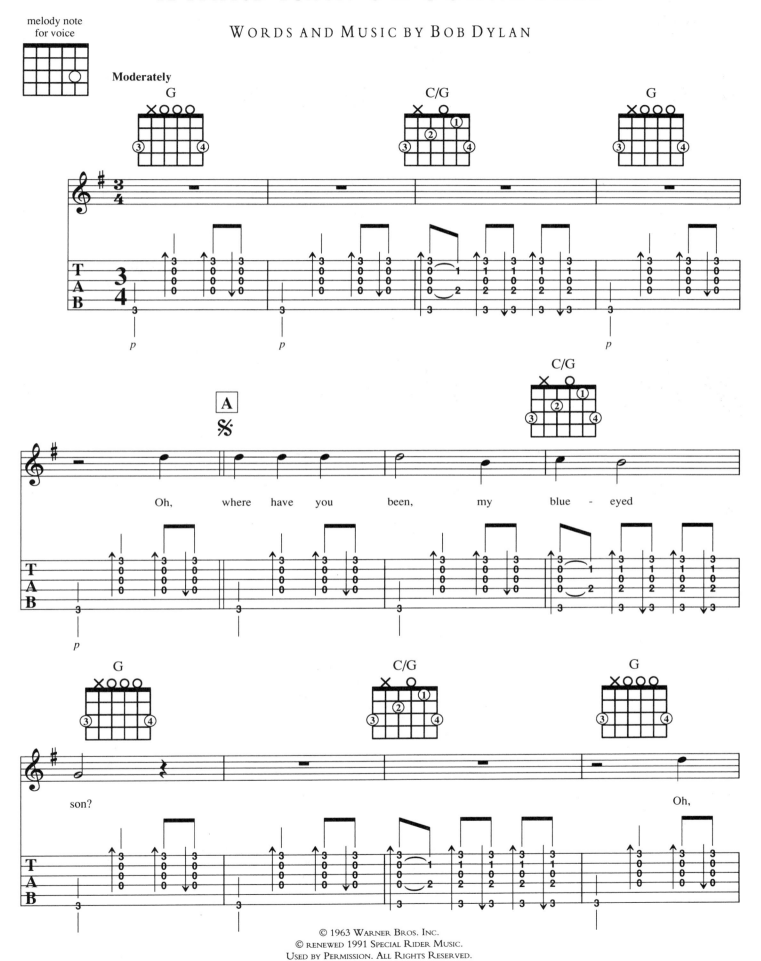

Oh, where have you been, my blue-eyed son? Oh,

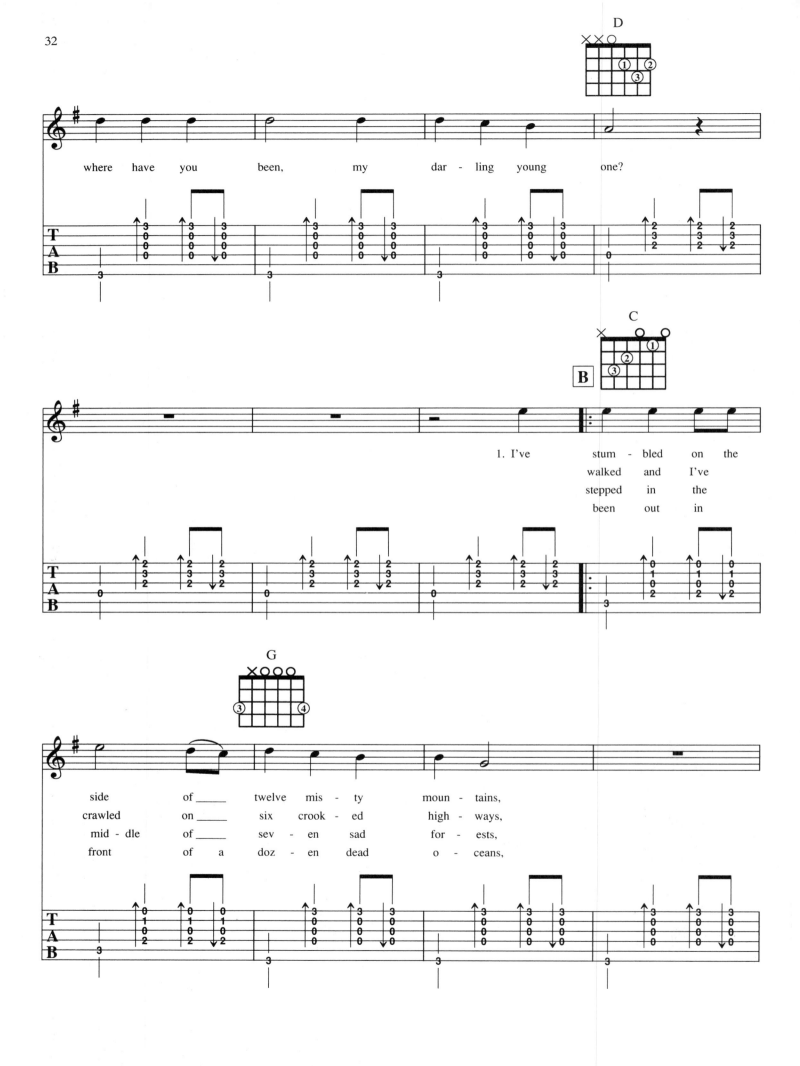

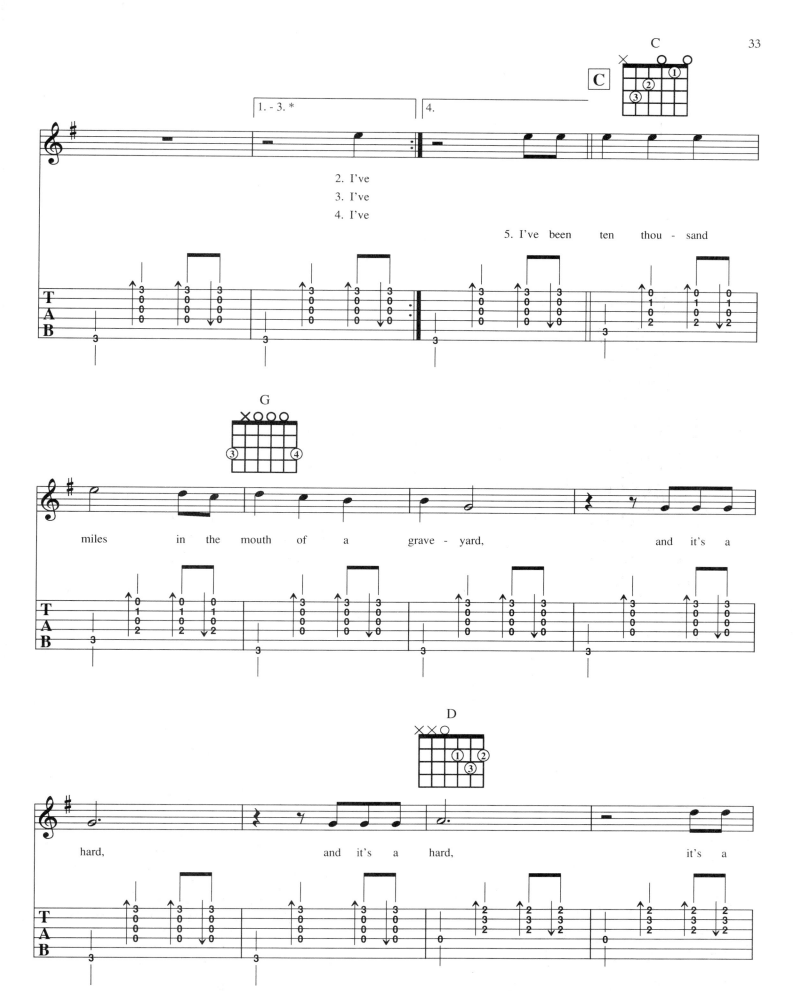

* Repeat as needed for additional lyrics.

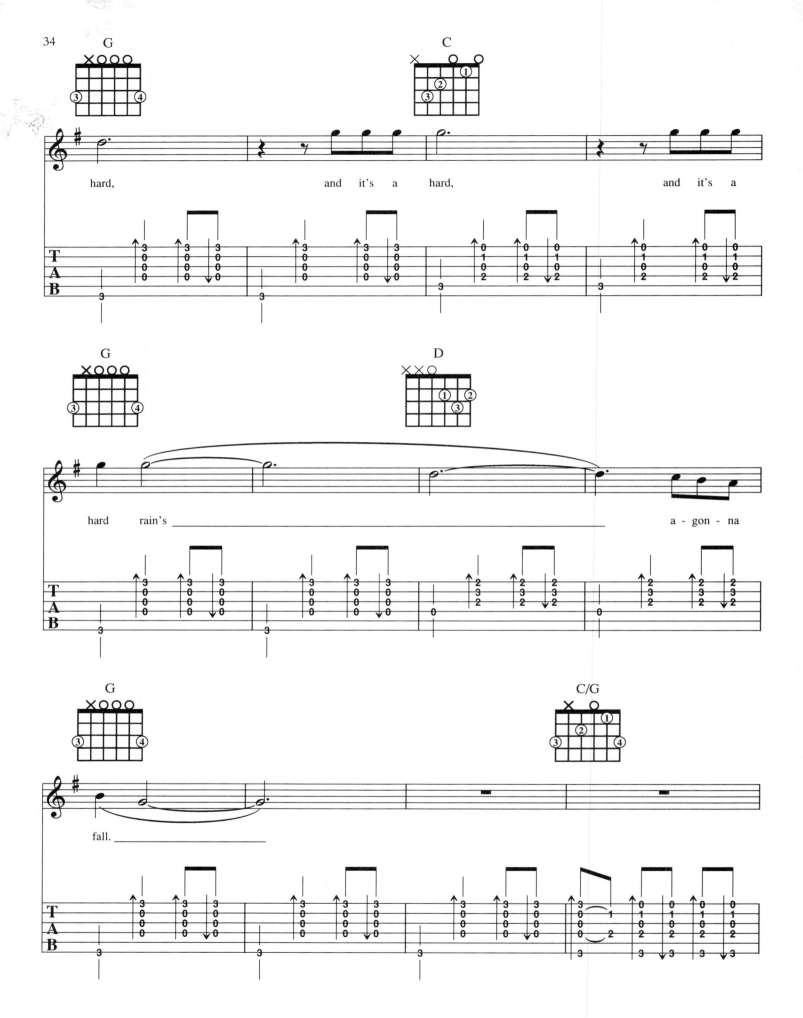

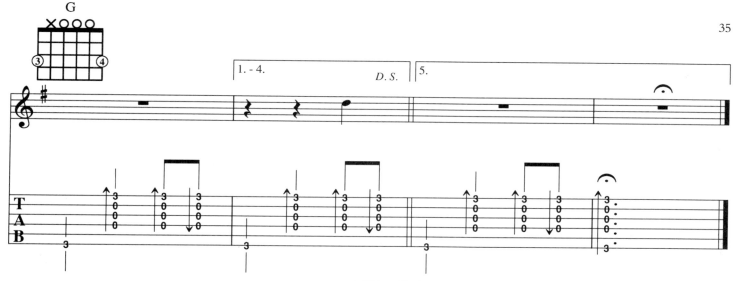

Additional lyrics

[A] Oh, what did you see, my blue eyed son?
Oh, what did you see, my darling young one?

[B] I saw a new born baby with wild wolves all around it,
I saw a highway of diamonds with nobody on it,
I saw a black branch with blood that kept drippin',
I saw a room full of men with their hammers a-bleedin',
I saw a white ladder all covered with water,
I saw ten thousand talkers whose tongues were all broken,

[C] I saw guns and sharp sword in the hands of young children,
And it's a hard, and it's a hard, it's a hard, it's a hard,
And it's a hard rain's a gonna fall.

[A] And what did you hear, my blue eyed son?
And what did you hear, my darling young one?

[B] I heard the sound of a thunder, it roared out a warnin',
Heard the roar of a wave that could drown the whole world,
Heard one hundred drummers whose hands were a-blazin',
Heard ten thousand whisperin' and nobody listenin',
Heard one person starve, I heard many people laughin',
Heard the song of a poet who died in the gutter,

[C] Heard the sound of a clown who cried in the alley,
And it's a hard, and it's a hard, it's a hard, it's a hard,
And it's a hard rain's a-gonna fall.

[A] Oh, who did you meet, my blue eyed son?
Who did you meet, my darling young one?

[B] I met a young child beside a dead pony,
I met a white man who walked a black dog,
I met a young woman whose body was burning,
I met a young girl, she gave me a rainbow,
I met one man who was wounded in love,

[C] I met another man who was wounded with hatred,
And it's a hard, it's a hard, it's a hard, it's a hard,
It's a hard rain's a-gonna fall.

[A] Oh, what'll you do now, my blue-eyed son?
Oh, what'll you do now, my darling young one?

[B] I'm a-goin' back out 'fore the rain starts a-fallin',
I'll walk to the depths of the deepest black forest,
Where the people are many and their hands are all empty,
Where the pellets of poison are flooding their waters,
Where the home in the valley meets the damp dirty prison,
Where the executioner's face is always well hidden,
Where hunger is ugly, where souls are forgotten,
Where black is the color, where none is the number,
And I'll tell it and think it and speak it and breathe it,
And reflect it from the mountain so all souls can see it,
Then I'll stand on the ocean until I start sinkin',

[C] But I'll know my song well before I start singin',
And it's a hard, it's a hard, it's a hard, it's a hard,
It's a hard rain's a gonna fall.

Only A Pawn In Their Game

Words and Music by Bob Dylan

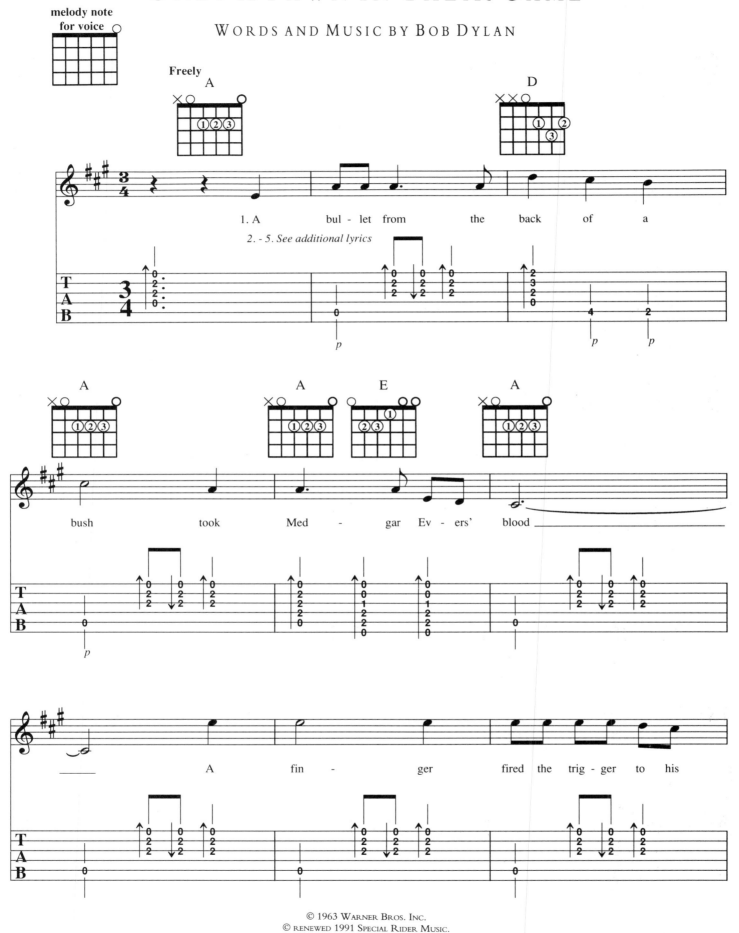

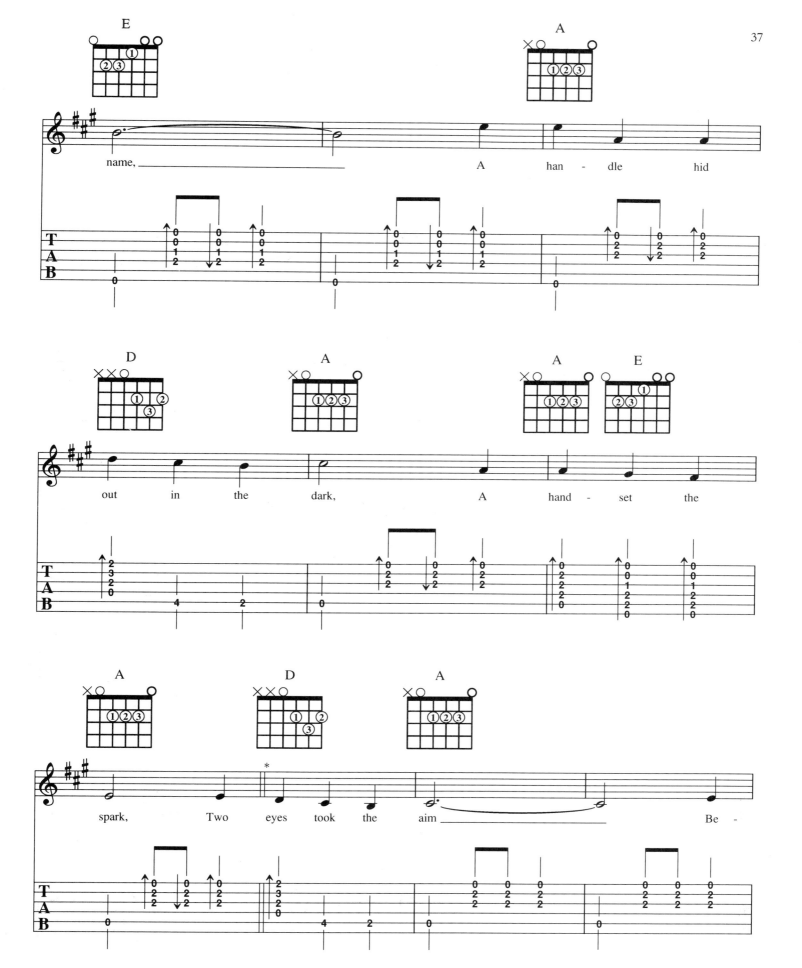

This section will vary in length to accomodate the additional lyrics.

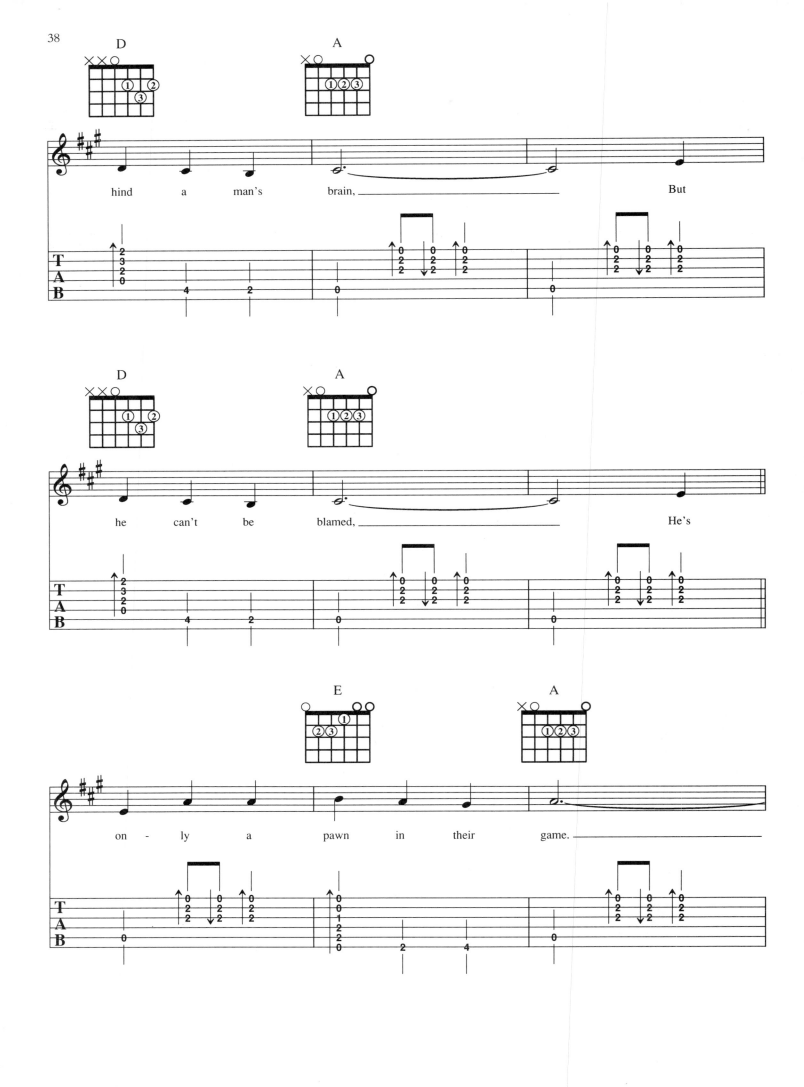

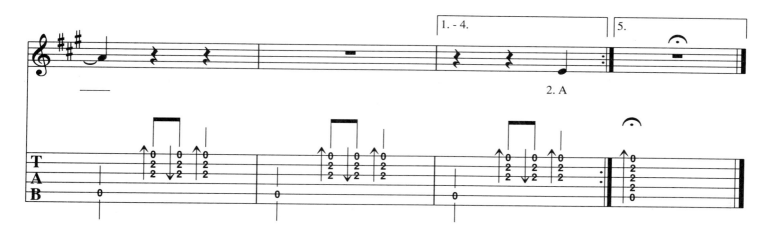

Additional lyrics

2. A South politician preaches to the poor, white man,
   You got more than the blacks, don't complain.
   You're better than them, you been born with white skin, they explain,
   And the Negro is named,
               * Is used it is plain,
                 For the politician's gain,
                 As he rises to fame,
                 And the poor white remains,
                 On the caboose of the train,
                 But it ain't him to blame,
   He's only a pawn in their game.

3. The deputy sheriffs, the soldiers, the governors get paid,
   And the marshals and cops get the same,
   But the poor white man's used in the hands of them all like a tool,
   He's taught in his school
               * From the start by the rule
                 That the laws are with him
                 To protect his white skin,
                 To keep up his hate
                 So he never thinks straight,
                 'Bout the shape that he's in,
                 But it ain't him to blame,
   He's only a pawn in their game.

4. From the poverty shacks he looks from the cracks to the tracks,
   And the hoof beats pound in his brain.
   And he's taught how to walk in a pack,
   Shoot in the back,
               * With his fist in a clinch,
                 To hang and to lynch,
                 To hide 'neath the hood,
                 To kill with no pain
                 Like a dog on a chain,
                 He ain't got no name
                 But it ain't him to blame,
   He's only a pawn in their game.

5. Today Medgar Evers was buried from the bullet he caught,
   They lowered him down as a king.
   But when the shadowy sun sets on the one
   That fired the gun,
               * He'll see by his grave
                 On the stone that remains,
                 Carved nest to his name
                 His epitaph plain;
   Only a pawn in their game.

Girl Of The North Country

Words and Music by Bob Dylan

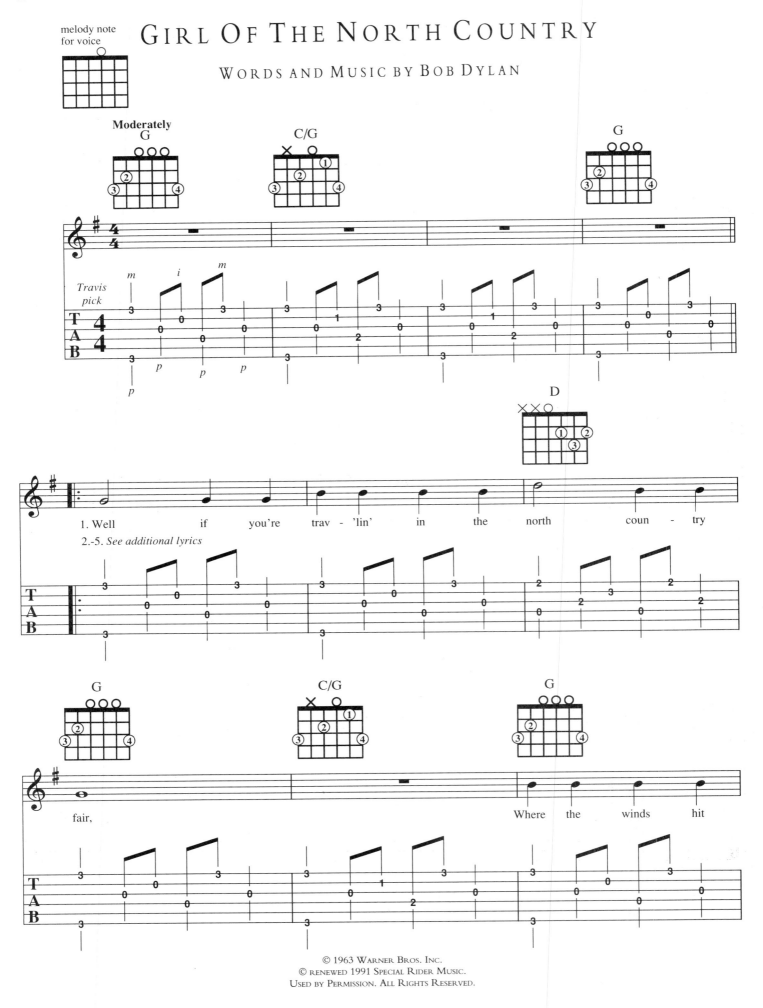

1. Well if you're trav-'lin' in the north coun-try

2.-5. *See additional lyrics*

fair,

Where the winds hit

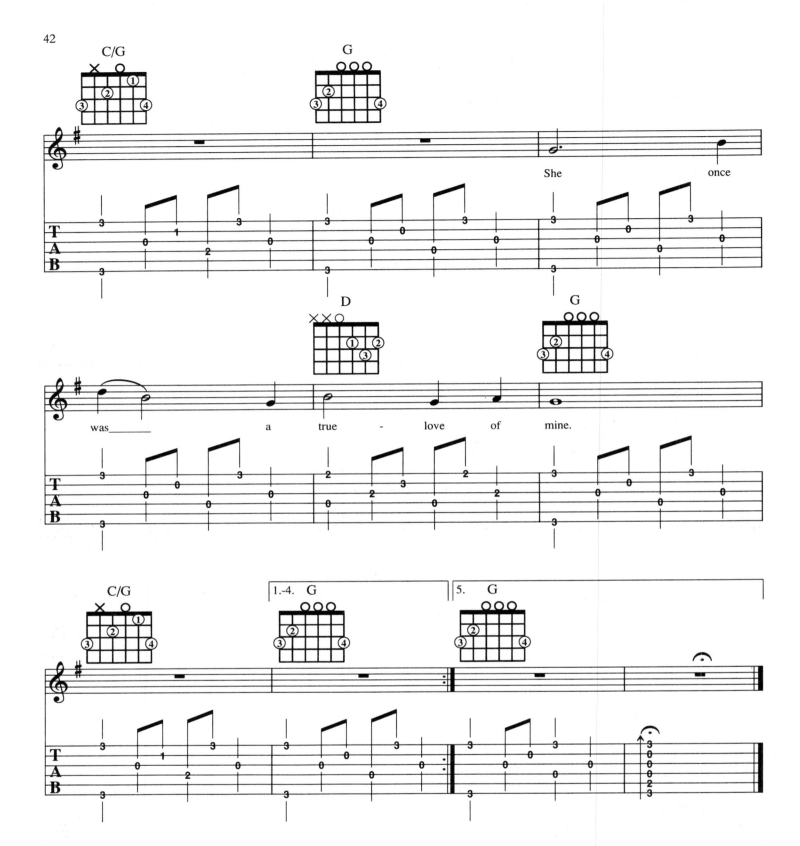

Additional lyrics

2. Well if you go in the snowflake storm
   When the rivers freeze and summer ends,
   Please see if she's wearing a coat so warm
   To keep her from the howlin' winds.

3. Please see for me if her hair hangs long,
   If it rolls and flows all down her breast.
   Please see for me her hair hangs long,
   That's the way I remember her best.

4. I'm a wonderin' if she remembers me at all,
   Many times I've often prayed
   In the darkness of my night,
   In the brightness of my day.

5. So if you're travelin' in the north country fair,
   Where the winds hit heavy on the borderline,
   Remember me to one who lives there,
   She once was a truelove of mine.

I Shall Be Released

Words and Music by Bob Dylan

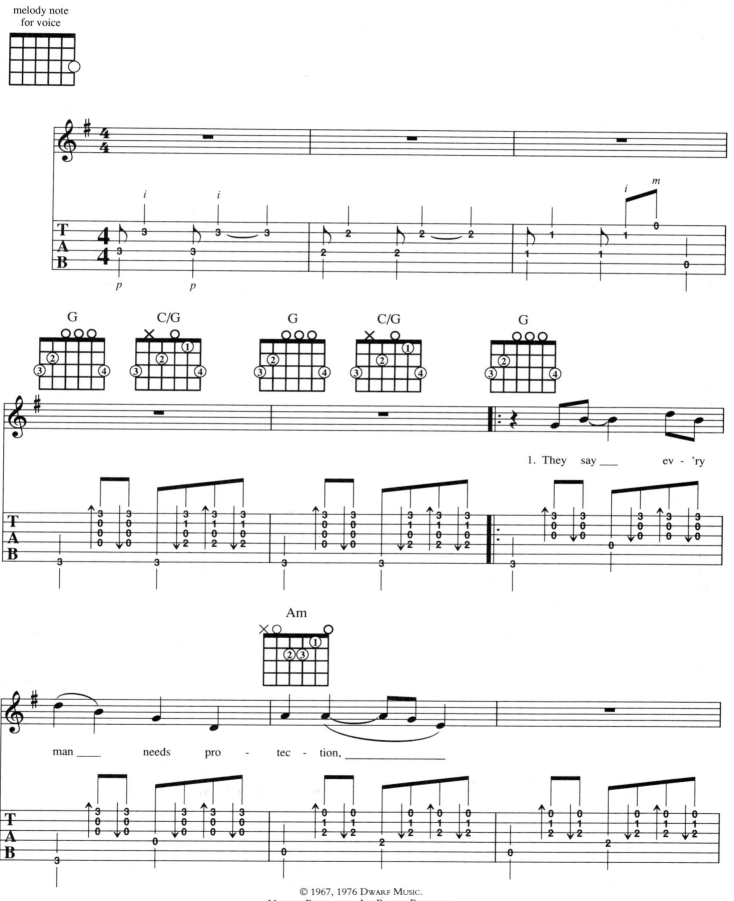

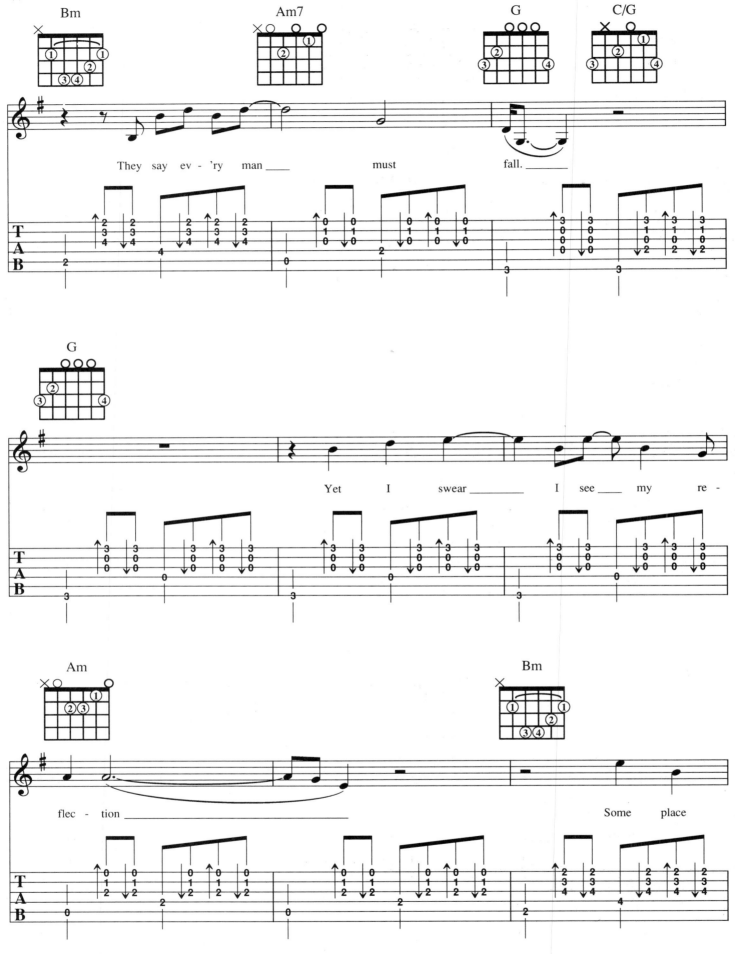

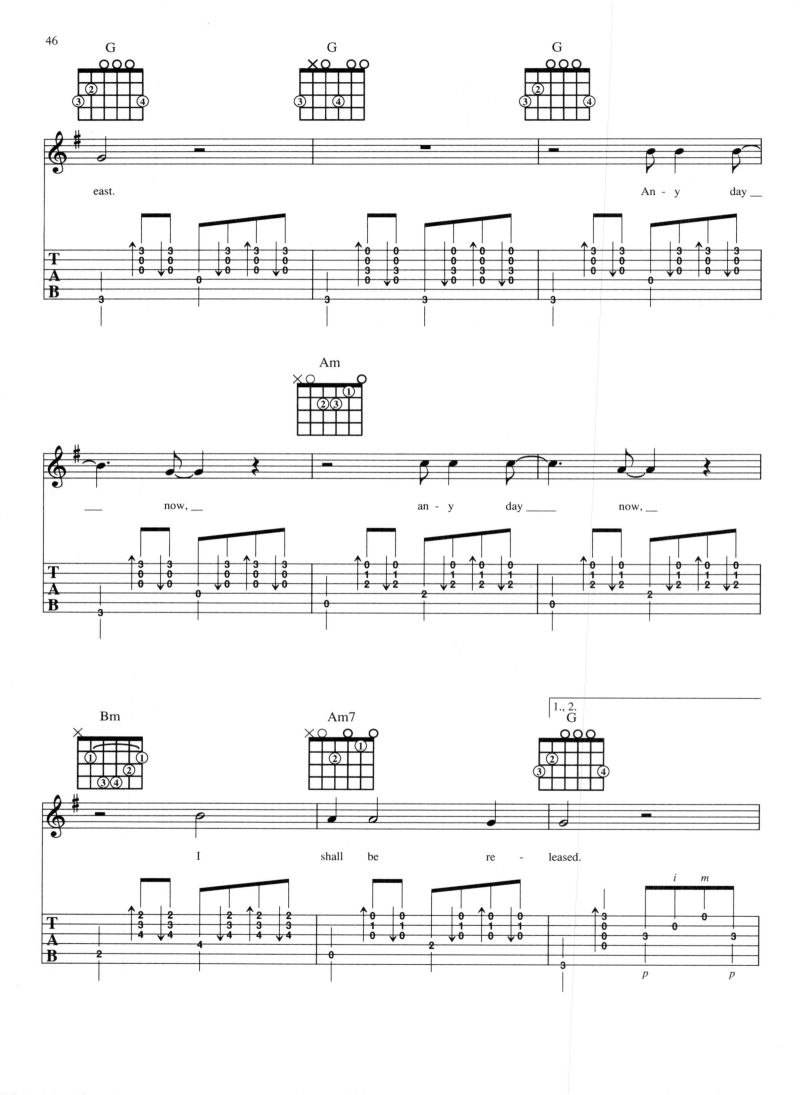

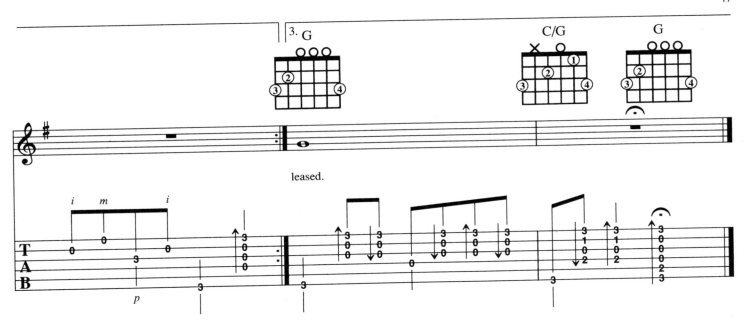

leased.

Additional lyrics

2. Standing next to me in this lonely crowd,
   Is a man who swears he's not to blame.
   All day long I hear him shout so loud,
   Crying out that he's been framed.

   Chorus

3. They say ev'rything can be replaced,
   Yet ev'ry distance is not near.
   So I remember ev'ry face
   Of ev'ry man who put me here.

   Chorus

MASTERS OF WAR

WORDS AND MUSIC BY BOB DYLAN

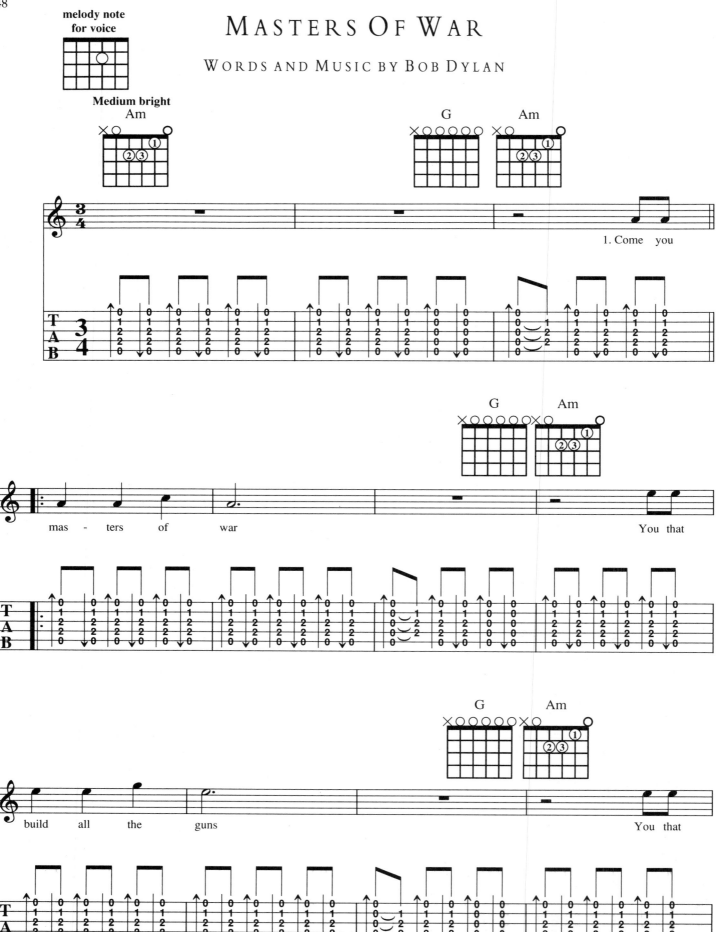

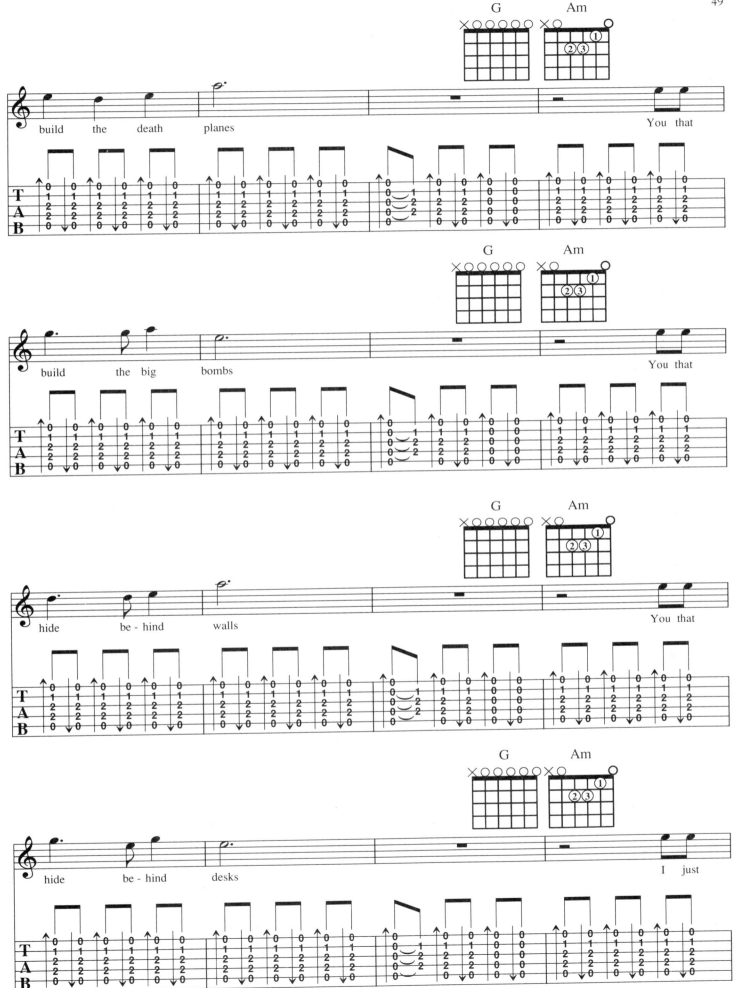

50

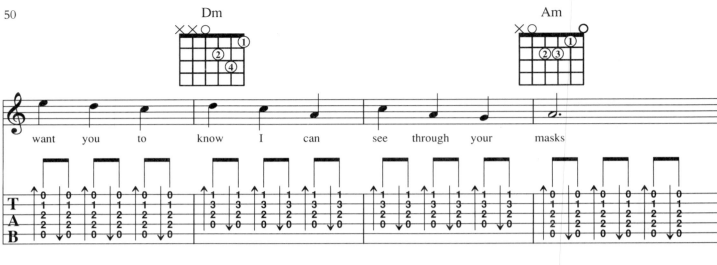

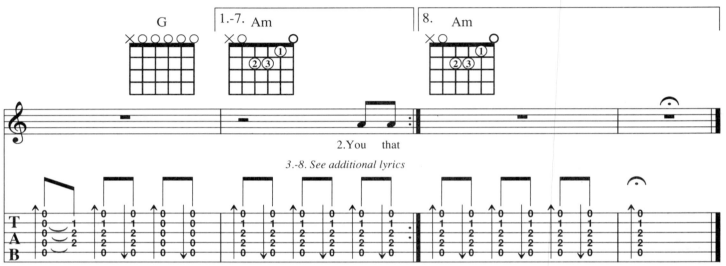

Additional lyrics

2. You that never done nothin'
   But build to destroy
   You play with my world
   Like it's your little toy
   You put a gun in my hand
   And you hide from my eyes
   And you turn and run farther
   When the fast bullets fly

3. Like Judas of old
   You lie and deceive
   A world war can be won
   You want me to believe
   But I see through your eyes
   And I see through your brain
   Like I see through the water
   That runs down my drain

4. You fasten the triggers
   For the others to fire
   Then you set back and watch
   When the death count gets higher
   You hide in your mansion
   As young people's blood
   Flows out of their bodies
   And is buried in the mud

5. You've thrown the worst fear
   That can ever be hurled
   Fear to bring children
   Into the world
   For threatenin' my baby
   Unborn and unnamed
   You ain't worth the blood
   That runs in your veins

6. How much do I know
   To talk out of turn
   You might say that I'm young
   You might say I'm unlearned
   But there's one thing I know
   Though I'm younger than you
   Even Jesus would never
   Forgive what you do

7. Let me ask you one question
   Is your money that good
   Will it buy you forgiveness
   Do you think that it could
   I think you will find
   When your death takes its toll
   All the money you made
   Will never buy back your soul

8. And I hope that you die
   And your death'll come soon
   I will follow your casket
   On a pale afternoon
   And I'll watch while you're lowered
   Down to your death bed
   And I'll stand o'er your grave
   'Till I'm sure that you're dead.

melody note
for voice

Tangled Up In Blue

Words and Music by Bob Dylan

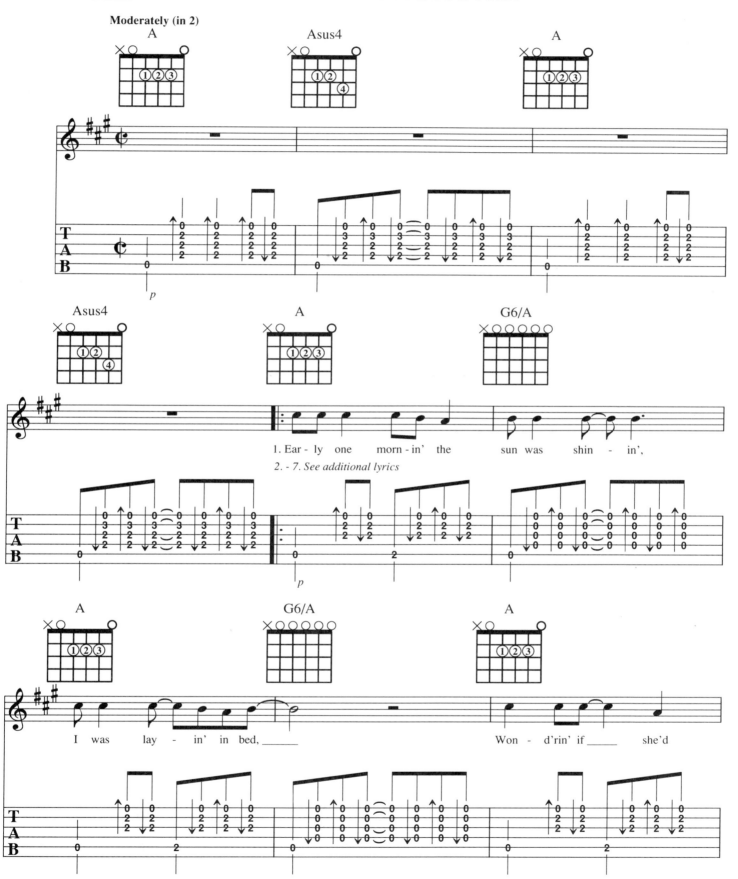

1. Ear - ly one morn - in' the sun was shin - in',

2. - 7. See additional lyrics

I was lay - in' in bed, _____ Won - d'rin' if _____ she'd

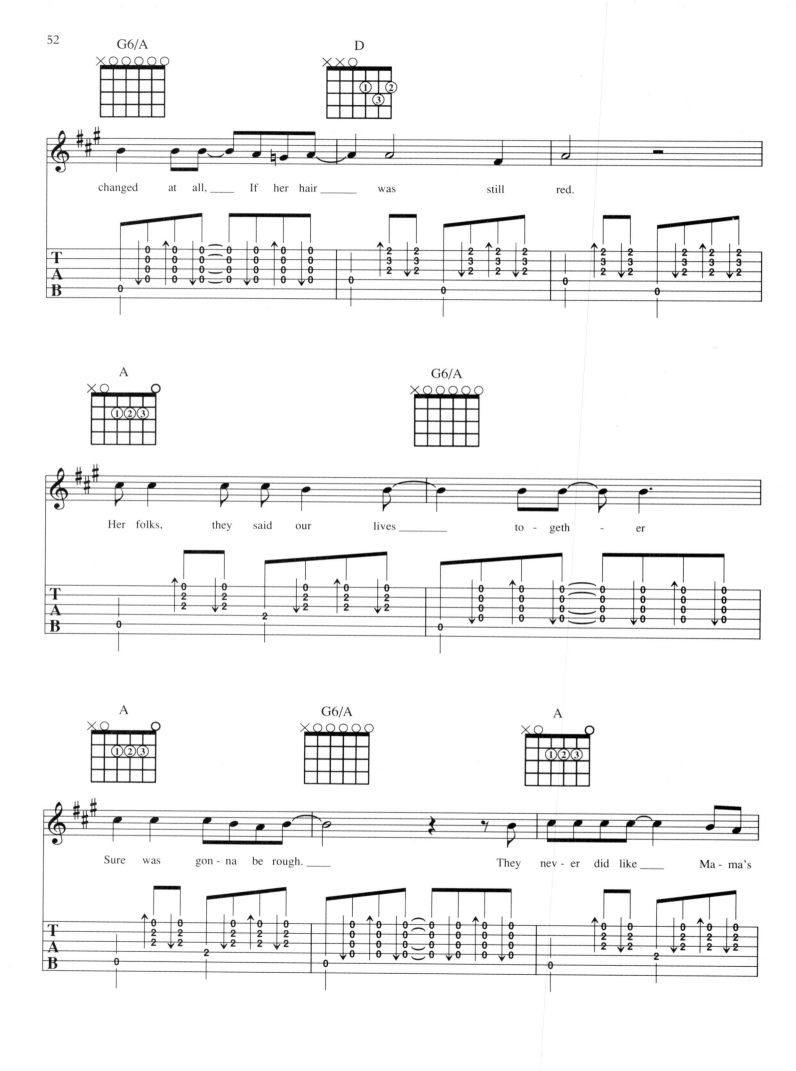

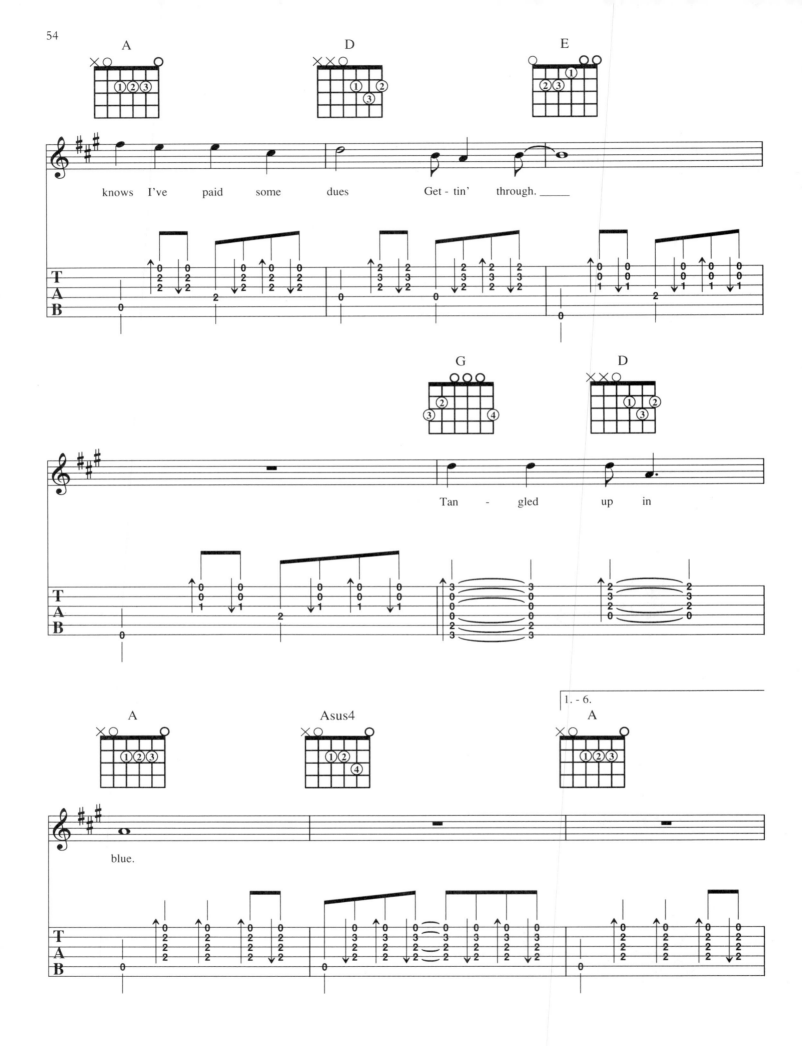

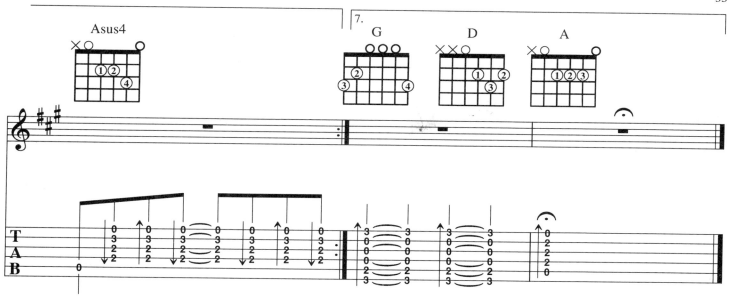

Additional lyrics

2. She was married when we first met,
   Soon to be divorced.
   I helped her out of a jam, I guess,
   But I used a little too much force.
   We drove that car as far as we could,
   Abandoned it out West.
   Split up on a dark sad night,
   Both agreeing it was best.
   She turned around to look at me,
   As I was walkin' away.
   I heard her say over my shoulder,
   "We'll meet again some day
   on the avenue."
   Tangled up in blue.

3. I had a job in the great north woods,
   Working as a cook for a spell.
   But I never did like it all that much,
   And one day the axe just fell.
   So I drifted down to New Orleans,
   Where I happened to be employed.
   Workin' for a while on a fishin' boat,
   Right outside of Delacroix.
   But all the while I was alone,
   The past was close behind.
   I seen a lot of women,
   But she never escaped my mind,
   And I just grew.
   Tangled up in blue.

4. She was workin' in a topless place,
   And I stopped in for a beer.
   I just kept lookin' at the side of her face,
   In the spotlight so clear.
   And later on as the crowd thinned out,
   I's just about to do the same.
   She was standing there in back of my chair,
   Said to me, "Don't I know your name?"
   I muttered somethin' underneath my breath,
   She studied the lines on my face.
   I must admit I felt a little uneasy,
   When she bent down to tie the laces
   Of my shoe.
   Tangled up in blue.

5. She lit a burner on the stove,
   And offered me a pipe.
   "I thought you'd never say hello," she said,
   "You look like the silent type."
   Then she opened up a book of poems,
   And handed it to me.
   Written by an Italian poet
   From the thirteenth century.
   And every one of them words rang true,
   And glowed like burnin' coal.
   Pourin' off of every page,
   Like it was written in my soul
   From me to you.
   Tangled up in blue.

6. I lived with them on Montague Street,
   In a basement down the stairs.
   There was music in the cafes at night,
   And revolution in the air.
   Then he started into dealing with slaves,
   And something inside of him died.
   She had to sell everything she owned,
   And froze up inside.
   And when finally the bottom fell out,
   I became withdrawn,
   The only thing I knew how to do,
   Was to keep on keepin' on,
   Like a bird that flew.
   Tangled up in blue.

7. So now I'm goin' back again,
   I got to get to her somehow.
   All the people we used to know,
   They're an illusion to me now.
   Some are mathematicians,
   Some are carpenters' wives.
   Don't know how it all got started,
   I don't know what they're doin' with their lives.
   But me, I'm still on the road,
   Headin' for another joint.
   We always did feel the same,
   We just saw it from a different point
   Of view.
   Tangled up in blue.

JUST LIKE A WOMAN

WORDS AND MUSIC BY BOB DYLAN

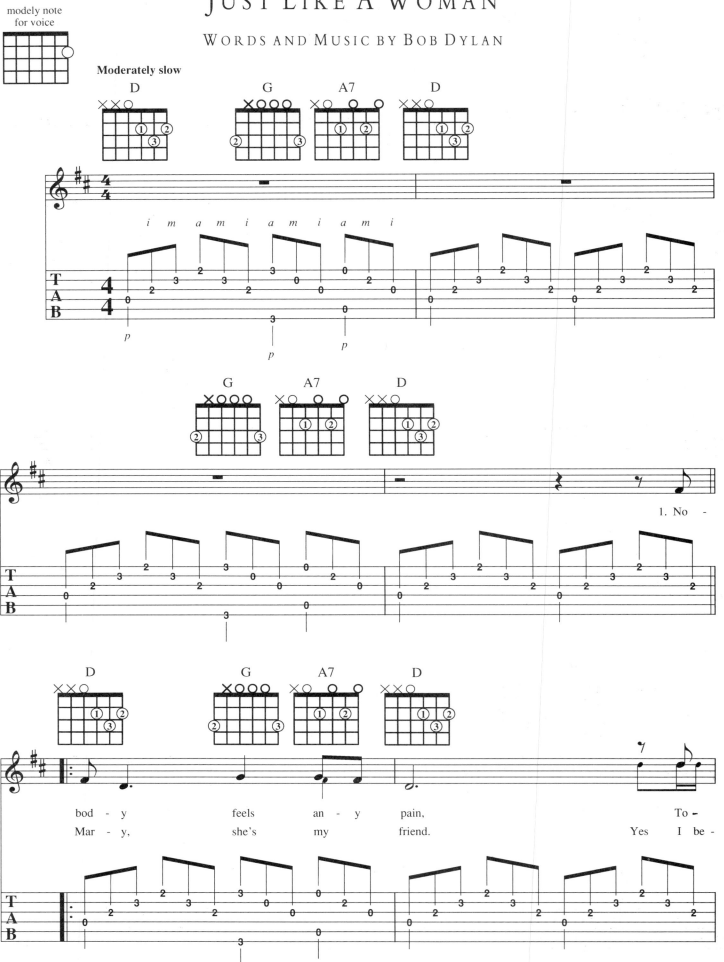

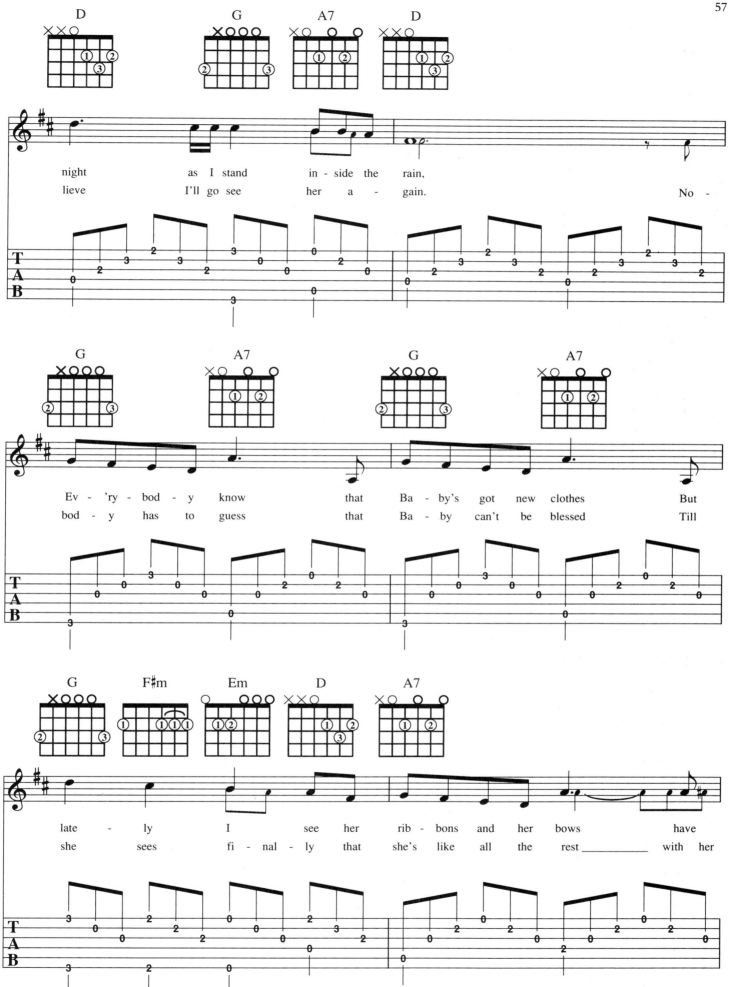

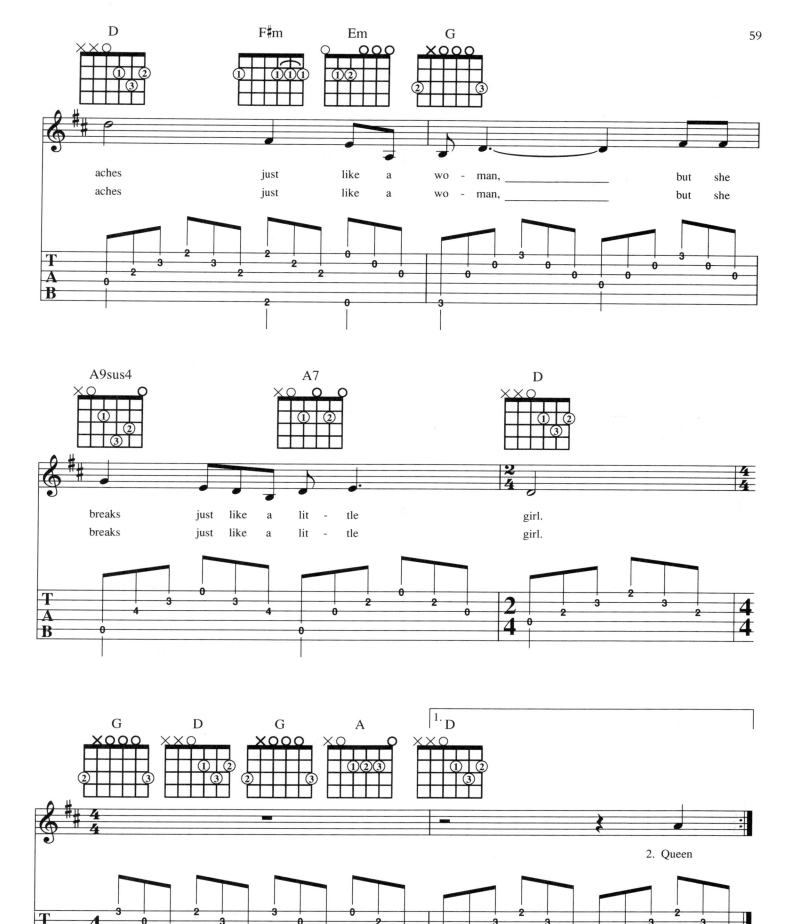

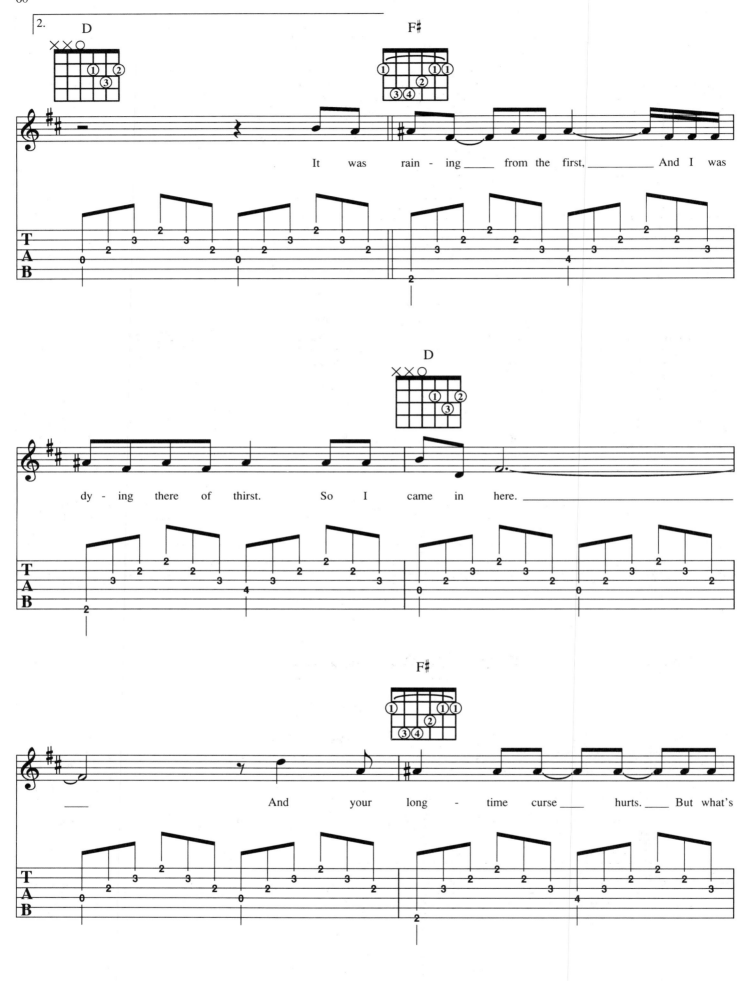

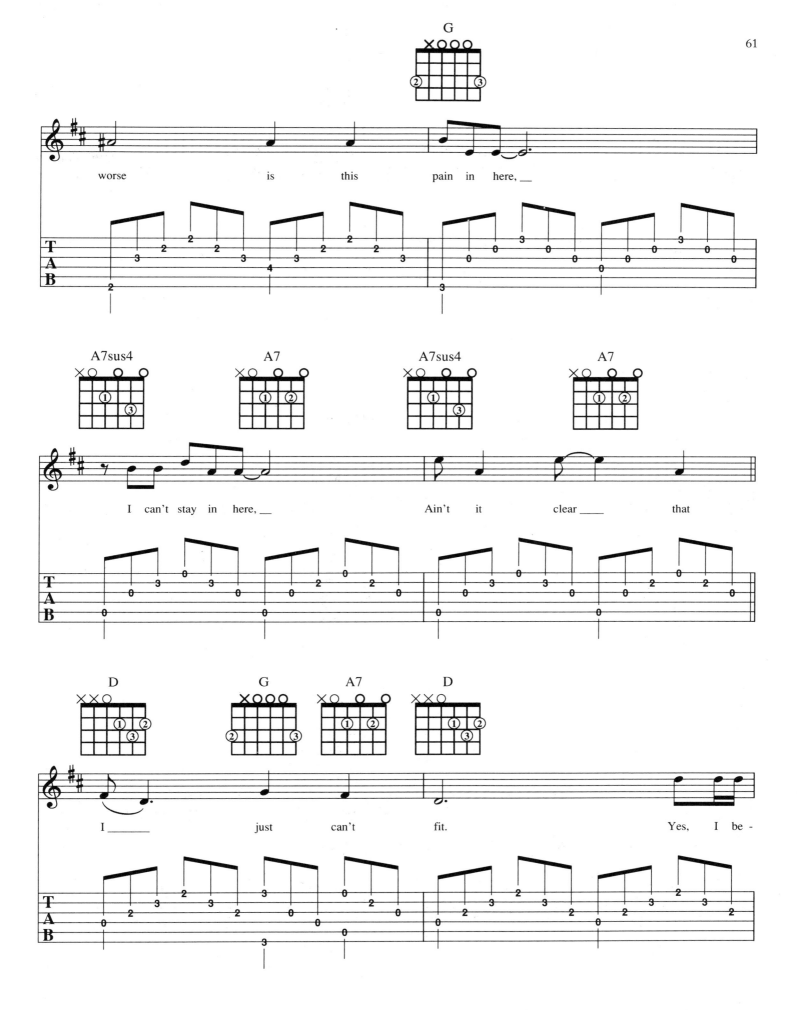

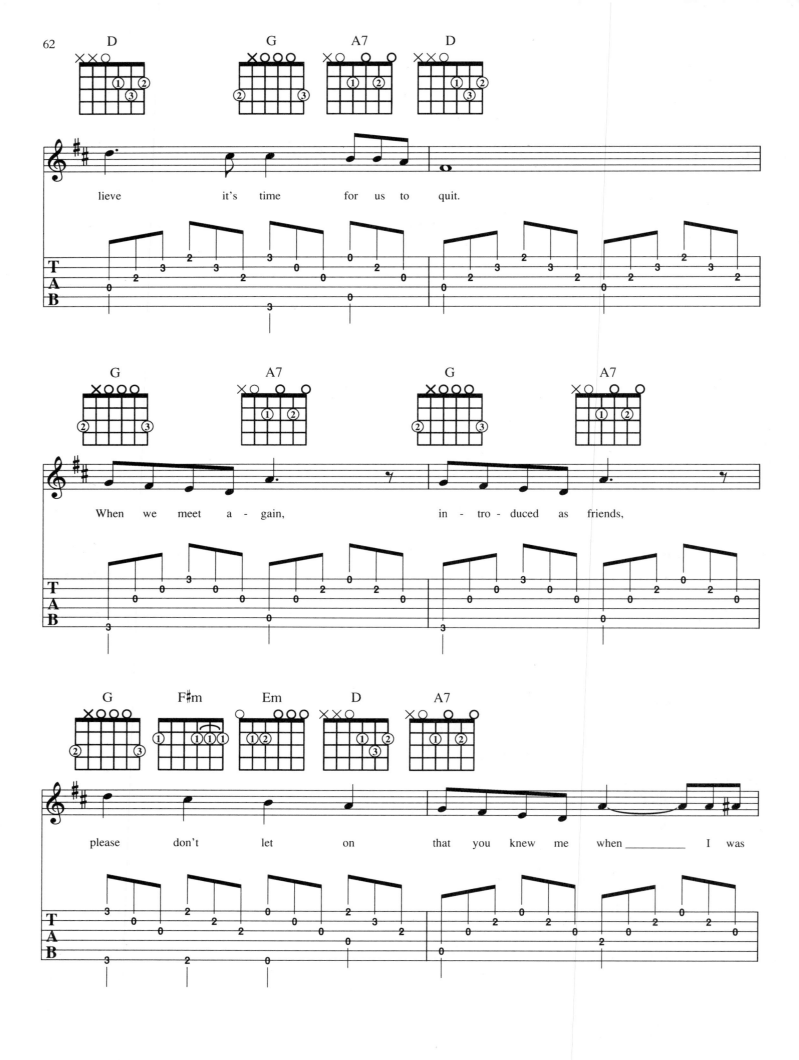

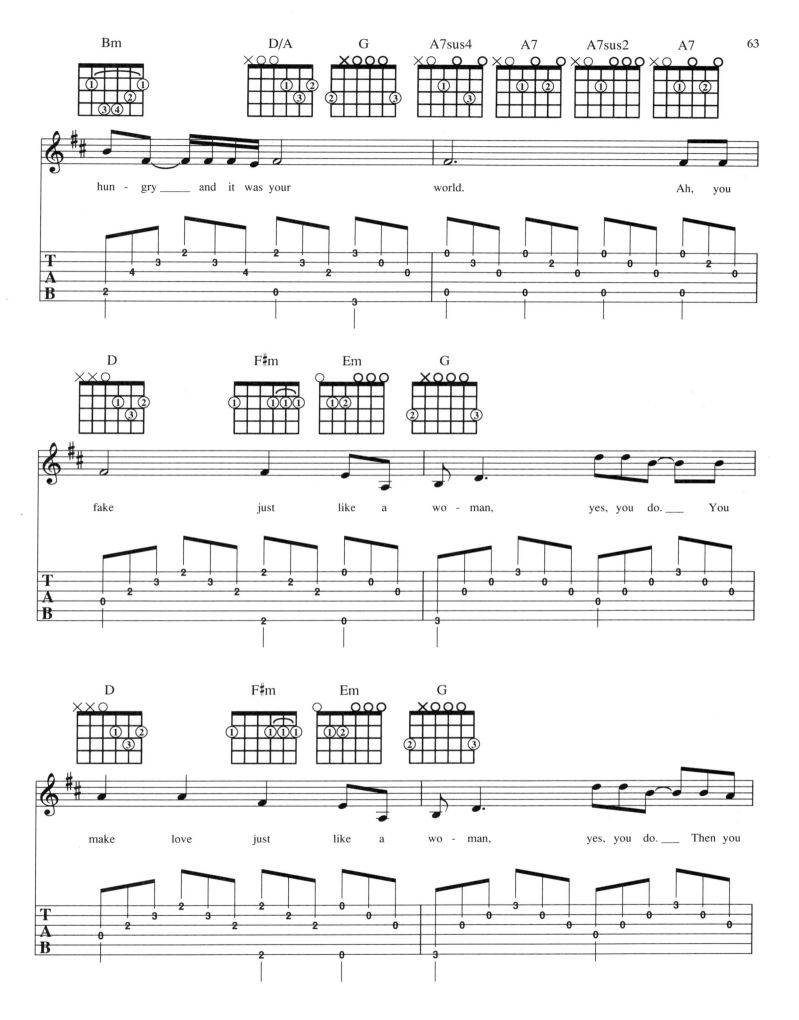

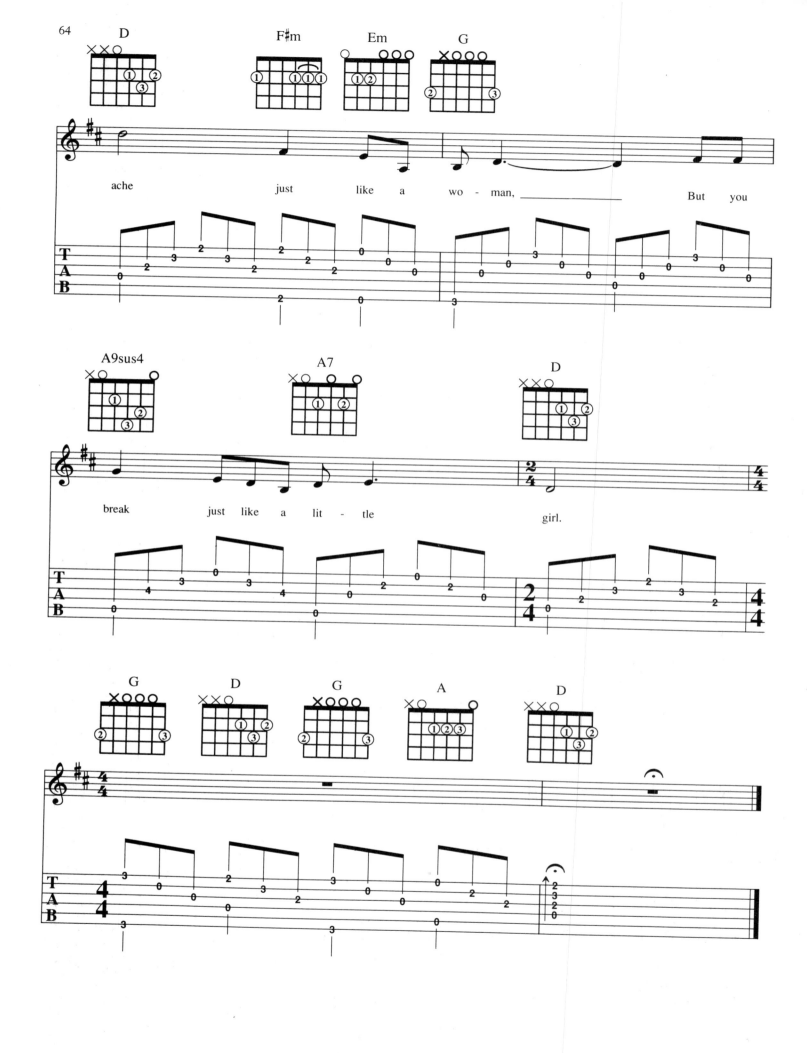